...ies of water and swift streams. But they require huge
...antities of fodder and eat as much as two camel caravans."

"I wondered how an elephant and a rhinoceros would behave
f brought face to face. As the mahouts continued to press

"One of the animals peculiar to India
is the elephant, which the Indians call Hati.
The elephant is an animal with a huge body
and keen intelligence.
It understands everything one says to it
and does everything it is told to do."

'In Indian armies, divisions that possess elephants go into battle
with them. Laden with heavy burdens, they can easily negotiate

forward, the rhinoceros did not stand its ground but fled in
another direction."

At Agra: "Before the meal, as I was being presented with gifts,
here was a match between enraged camels and elephants on the

island across from us. There were also fights between rams. Then
it was the wrestlers' turn to fight."

Babur often deployed elephants alongside his cavalry.

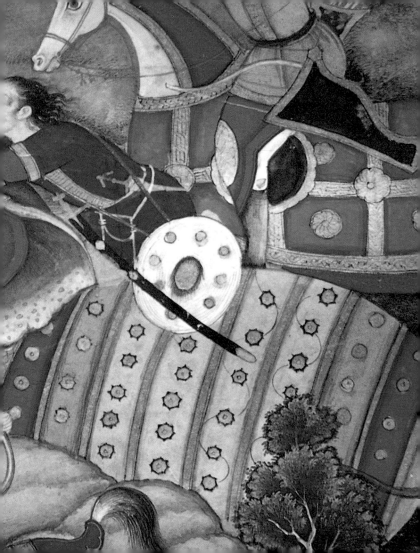

CONTENTS

THE LIFE AND LORE
OF THE ELEPHANT

Robert Delort

THAMES AND HUDSON

"Some woolly mammoths brought the Ulhamrs to a halt. They were foraging, tearing out soft vegetation, digging up roots; to the three men their existence seemed happy, secure and magnificent. Beneath their huge feet, a giant lion would be so much clay; their tusks could uproot oaks, their granite-like heads could smash them to bits. As he contemplated the suppleness of their trunks, Naoh could not help saying, 'The mammoth is master over all life on earth!'"

J.H. Rosny, *Quest for Fire*, 1911

CHAPTER 1
THE ELEPHANT FAMILY

The classic image of the woolly mammoth (left), set in the tundra over ten thousand years ago. Right: an elephant calf.

The family album: it all starts in Egypt

Living elephants are the descendants of a fairly small tapir-like mammal that lived at least 45 million years ago: *Moeritherium*, named after Egypt's Lake Moeris, near which its remains were discovered. Its enlarged incisors had already developed into rudimentary tusks, two in each jaw. Although most of its evolutionary offshoots have since died out, they left behind a wealth of fossil remains that have been studied in considerable detail.

Primelephas gave rise to the Elephantoidea, the most recent of proboscidean families and the only one to witness the emergence of *Homo sapiens*. In the course of their development, 'dwarf' forms (such as the Maltese elephant) and certain mammoths, which also may have died out as dwarf species in the Siberian Arctic, became extinct. The sole survivors were the woolly mammoth (*Mammuthus primigenius*), its close relative, the Asian elephant (*Elephas maximus*), and the more distinctive African elephant (*Loxodonta africana*). All three were the products of roughly the same evolutionary process. As their heads became massive, lighter, spongier bone tissue and stronger neck muscles were developed; additional tusks were lost (the lower jaw could not support their weight, so they would have been left perpetually open-mouthed); and the nose and upper lip lengthened into a heavy, muscular trunk.

*M*oeritherium and a sampling of its lineage, below. (Left to right: *Moeritherium*, *Phiomia*, *Palaeomastodon*, *Gomphotherium*, *Deinotherium*, *Mastodon*, *Mammuthus*, *Loxodonta*.) Actual body sizes differed from those shown: *Moeritherium* was one-sixth or one-seventh the size of the mastodon, itself bigger than the mammoth and the African elephant. There were several distinct evolutionary lines. Scientists in the 19th century named the Deinotherioidea after their last representative, a four-tusker they considered so terrible (*deinos*) in appearance they called it *Deinotherium*. The Elephantoidea include the Gomphotherioidea (*gomphos* = 'bolt', thus 'stiff', and *therion* = 'wild animal').

A lumbering grandparent: the woolly mammoth

The woolly mammoth is the best known of all prehistoric animals, more so than the woolly rhinoceros, the sabre-toothed tiger, the cave bear or the urus, an extinct longhorned wild ox. There are several reasons for this. This strange-looking beast was at least as big as an African elephant but it looked not only taller because of its high, domed head, but also more massive (its fur, more than 0.7 metres long, swelled its rounded bulk) and heavier (it weighed about 7 metric tons). Its tusks, which could spiral into an almost complete circle, measured up to about 5 metres and weighed up to 125 kilos each!

The woolly mammoth was well established in various cultures of Siberia and, probably through these peoples, in China, where use of its bluish

The woolly mammoth frequently appears in prehistoric cave paintings, such as this one from Pech-Merle, France. Of particular interest in this splendid silhouette is the steep upward slope from the hindquarters to the crown of the head.

ivory – the so-called 'teeth of the Tien-shu rat' goes back thousands of years. According to a Chinese description said to date from the 5th century BC, this dull-witted, sluggish 'rat' the size of an ox or buffalo supposedly lived underground and died the moment it saw the light of the sun or the moon. Its neck was thought to be short, its eyes small, its tail no more than a foot long. In the West woolly mammoths were frequently depicted in cave paintings and later popularized in *Quest for Fire* (1911) and other novels.

Why did the woolly mammoth die out?

Recent Soviet investigators have tended to extend the woolly mammoth's evolutionary lifespan. They maintain that the very last representatives of the species, ranging throughout northeastern Siberia or even Alaska, may have died out not some ten thousand years ago, but scarcely five thousand years ago, around the time of the first Egyptian dynasties. The explanations for their extinction are many and varied; the widely divergent hypotheses reflect the prevailing

Woolly mammoths as they lived (above) and as they were found in Siberia some ten thousand years later. A Dutchman named Witsen is said to have coined the word 'mammoth' in 1692 after a trip to Muscovy. Although its exact etymology is unknown, in Estonian *maa* and *mutt* mean 'earth' and 'mole', respectively. (These beasts were thought to burrow in the earth like moles.)

attitudes of the time in which they were made.

Only lately have Soviet and American scientists stated the problem correctly: woolly mammoths, which were perfectly adapted to the cold, died out during a period of climatic warming. To be sure, hunting – by manoeuvring them over cliffs or trapping them in bogs – may have wiped out a substantial number of these lumbering beasts, which had an especially long breeding cycle. This may have spurred herds to move northeast, in the same direction as the retreating glaciers; but the coniferous forest belt, taiga, was also edging northwards, wedging the treeless tundra between it and the Arctic Ocean.

The mammoths may have finally been trapped by the taiga, especially as heavier snow cover and extensive summer thawing would have inundated available forage, debilitated herds and prevented mothers from protecting and feeding their young. Ever-shrinking grazing grounds, a brief recurrence of cold conditions and predation by human populations has been well documented in Alaska around the 9th millennium BC.

In 1799 a huge mammoth was found in Siberia and an eminent scientist by the name of Adams had its skeleton, tusks, fur and hide fragments transported to St Petersburg. Subsequent discoveries, the most famous of which occurred in 1900, were documented on record cards that were updated with each new find. Scientists were thus able to distinguish among several types of mammoth, including 'dwarfs' the size of the living forest elephant. Their celebrated tusks measured just under 4.8 metres long and weighed 125 kilos each.

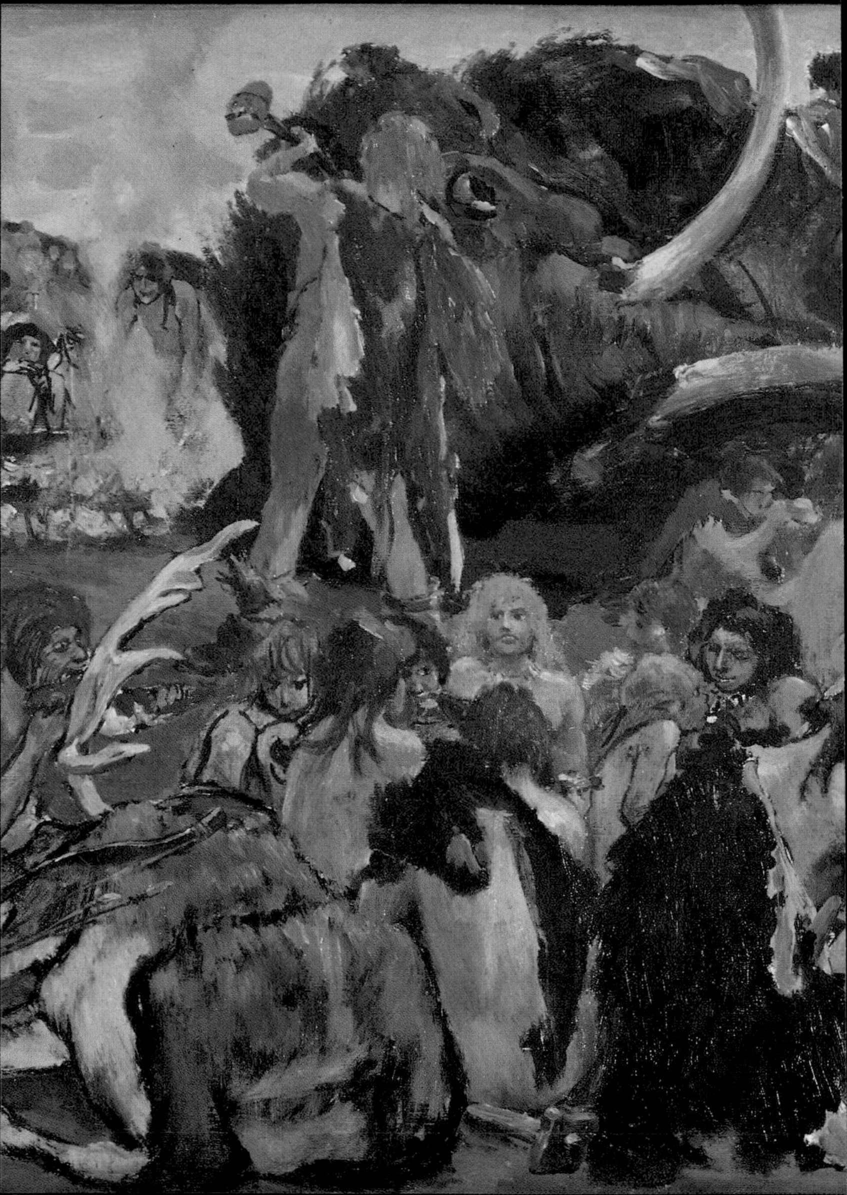

This re-creation of a mammoth hunt was based on techniques Africans use to hunt elephants and corroborated by archaeological finds. Experts on prehistoric human life have documented the use of the bow and arrow and traps as well as the manoeuvring of panic-stricken animals into incapacitating mud or over cliffs. The larger-than-life staging by Soviet realist Viktor Vasnetsov (1848–1926) depicts the wave of glee that presumably swept over (Neanderthal?) man once he got his hands on the 'mountain of meat'. Its other purposes notwithstanding, the clothing is intended to suggest a cold climate; hunters in the savanna (above) were believed to be completely naked.

These factors would have sealed the fate of the species and entombed a number of individuals in ice.

At the same time, the annual breakup of the slowly widening rivers would have conveyed bones, tusks, even fresh carcasses downstream by the scores or hundreds, piling them into bights and coves, where they remained, waiting to be discovered. One such deposit yielded dozens of tusks and more than eight thousand bones from over 120 individuals – a veritable graveyard.

African and Asian elephants: cousins and brothers

Only two species of elephant have survived since the extinction of the woolly mammoth: the Asian elephant (*Elephas maximus*) and the African elephant (*Loxodonta africana*).

The Asian elephant is smaller (seldom more than 3 metres tall) and not as heavy (rarely over 3 metric tons) though, older domesticated bull elephants have been known to stand well over 3 metres and weigh in excess of 4 tons. Its ears are relatively small, and its tusks are occasionally long and slender but more commonly short and light. But only 60 per cent of male Asian elephants carry tusks; all females are tuskless. It has one 'finger' at the tip of its trunk, an arched back and a domed forehead. Its skin is dark but may lighten with age and, in the case of exceedingly rare 'white' elephants, turn greyish-white. These are other physical,

Pictured here are the living elephants of Asia (right) and Africa (below), distant cousins. The most conspicuous differences are: ear size – huge in Africa, smaller in Asia; tusks on bulls – thick and turned up in Africa, slender and straighter in Asia; trunk – noticeably segmented, with two 'fingers' in Africa and less obviously ringed and single-fingered in Asia. The engraver tried to capture the 'retiring' disposition of the round-backed Indian elephant, whereas the pose and demeanour chosen by the painter for his impression of the African elephant convey a sense of power.

albeit less obvious, features: its molars, for example, are rasping surfaces with parallel ridges.

The African elephant is bigger (large bulls stand more than 3.5 metres tall; record height: 4.1 metres) and heavier, at 4 to 5 tons with record weights of up to 10 tons. Its ears are huge and spread out whenever it needs to shed heat or wants to intimidate an adversary by looking even more daunting than it already is. Its tusks, especially those of males, are long and thick; the heaviest ever found – 102.7 kilos – came from an elephant found on Mt Kilimanjaro. Its trunk is more conspicuously segmented than its Asian cousin's, and there are two finger-like 'lips' at the tip.

Its rump rises higher than its swayed back, and its head is broad and massive. Lastly, its molars have lozenge-shaped ridges (hence the genus name *Loxodonta*).

African elephants are divided into two distinct subspecies based on characteristic physical features. The bush elephant, *Loxodonta africana africana*, is bigger, has grey skin, and its front- and hindquarters are of equal height. Its tusks curve up and are quite long. The forest elephant is far more compact — bulls

For Europeans, elephants have long symbolized the exotic. They were even thought to roam America, where no one had ever actually seen an elephant — and certainly not in the imaginary form on the left.

and cows stand no more than about 2.4 and 1.95 metres tall, respectively — but still weighs in at a hefty 4 tons. Its short tusks, which grow almost straight or downwards are thick and heavy. Its head is lower, its back less concave. Its ears are almost circular instead of triangular; hence the name *Loxodonta africana cyclotis*, or 'round-eared'. Its dark, almost blackish, body looks nearly round, especially as the front part is slightly underslung.

In praise of the trunk, the elephant's strong and weak point

Obviously, the elephant's outstanding feature is its powerful yet flexible and sensitive trunk, which ends in one or two 'fingers'. This dexterous appendage has such a light touch it can pluck flowers, pick up a coin and

African or Asian, the elephant's outstanding physical characteristic is its ponderous, extremely sensitive trunk. When resting, the animal gladly parks this heavy load on its tusks, if it has any and during a charge the trunk is usually drawn in behind the tusks for protection. Tigers that dare to take on elephants have no alternative but to attempt to injure the trunk with their powerful claws. The tactic may not save the tiger's life, but it may jeopardize that of its foe (through haemorrhage infections).

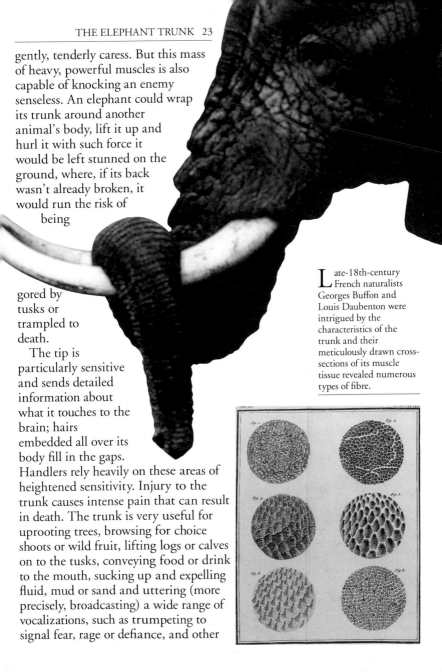

gently, tenderly caress. But this mass of heavy, powerful muscles is also capable of knocking an enemy senseless. An elephant could wrap its trunk around another animal's body, lift it up and hurl it with such force it would be left stunned on the ground, where, if its back wasn't already broken, it would run the risk of being

gored by tusks or trampled to death.

The tip is particularly sensitive and sends detailed information about what it touches to the brain; hairs embedded all over its body fill in the gaps. Handlers rely heavily on these areas of heightened sensitivity. Injury to the trunk causes intense pain that can result in death. The trunk is very useful for uprooting trees, browsing for choice shoots or wild fruit, lifting logs or calves on to the tusks, conveying food or drink to the mouth, sucking up and expelling fluid, mud or sand and uttering (more precisely, broadcasting) a wide range of vocalizations, such as trumpeting to signal fear, rage or defiance, and other

Late-18th-century French naturalists Georges Buffon and Louis Daubenton were intrigued by the characteristics of the trunk and their meticulously drawn cross-sections of its muscle tissue revealed numerous types of fibre.

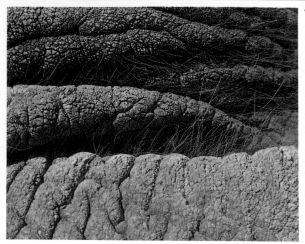

'Pachyderm' means 'thick-skinned', but an elephant's hide is not as thick as that of a rhinoceros. It owes its extreme sensitivity to the presence of numerous hairs. Its deep creases and wrinkles harbour a whole fauna of skin parasites that elephants find difficult to keep under control. Since its fly whisk of a tail is not long enough to help, whenever possible it must coat itself with dust or mud, take long, refreshing baths and rely on the services of the famous cattle egret, which operates with far more caution and delicacy than the oxpecker (which picks ticks with a vengeance and will take the liberty of pecking – and irritating – sores).

sounds directed at relatives, companions and friends. And, last but not least, it houses a keen sense of smell.

Head to toe

An elephant's eyes are small and easily dazzled in the open, but its vision improves in forest shadows. Its acute sense of hearing does not depend on the size of its ear flaps, which serve primarily as thermoregulatory devices. The temporal gland between the eye and ear periodically exudes a foul-smelling secretion that signals a period of heightened aggressiveness called musth (possibly, but not necessarily, in conjunction with the onset of the rut or oestrus) and is a sure sign of excitability or stress.

There are two types of teeth, molars and incisors. Tough vegetation wears down the huge, grinding

Veritable grating machines, the molars of elephants and their ancestors have distinctive surface configurations that make them easy to identify. Below left: mastodon tooth; below right and opposite: tooth and jaw from mammoths.

molars, but once they have lost their effectiveness, replacement sets of three premolars and three molars are in reserve, ready to push in from behind. After the sixth replacement the elephant, by then past fifty years of age, is no longer able to chew its food properly. Its diet now restricted to soft forage, it confines itself to marshlands, where it eventually wastes away and, succumbing to hunger and weakness, ends up sunk in the mud or finished off by predators. As a result, elephants in the wild infrequently live to sixty; in any event, their lifespan rarely exceeds that of people.

Another way to tell one species from another is by the toenails. As a rule, African elephants have four on the hind feet and five on the front; in Asia, the number can vary considerably from one individual to the next.

An elephant's tusks are, in fact, incisors that grow continuously throughout life, and in older bulls they are often very large indeed. If too long and heavy, they can become dangerous encumbrances, dragging on the ground, draining the animal of energy and minerals. Most of the time, however, they come in quite handy as tools for digging up soil, locating water under damp sand and even toting a ponderous trunk or clumsy calves. Sometimes they are used as jousting devices during friendly sparring or as a weapon in self-defence or while attacking (the trunk is then drawn in for protection until the moment of impact).

Finally, elephants have well-developed brains that weigh about 5 or 6 kilos, three to four times heavier than the human brain, albeit smaller in proportion to body size or weight. Their remarkable feet, which come equipped with sole pads that expand when weight is brought down on them and contract when pressure is

In 1803 the Dutch East India Company donated two Indian elephants, Hans and Parkie, to Holland. The couple soon became famous. They were captured by French troops and, despite local

released, are unsurpassed for negotiating marshland; they also enable the animal to tread smoothly and noiselessly. There are five toes on each foot, but the number of toenails can vary.

Elephant calves

A bull elephant can start breeding when it is only nine to twelve years old, but since adolescent males are banished from the family unit by mature females, they seldom get the chance to do so before the age of fifteen or twenty. Even then, they must often defer to a dominant bull who moves through the herd and impregnates receptive cows, usually during the rainy season (although, theoretically, females are in a state of quasiperpetual oestrus). In captivity bulls are isolated for a period of two to three weeks during the rutting season. Mating proper, which involves 'foreplay' of touching and caressing, is short-lived and is followed by thirty seconds or so of actual copulation and two to three days of communal living. Occasionally the dominant bull will drift away so quickly that younger males take advantage of a receptive female even

opposition, escorted to Paris. Gawking observers and scientists crowded round to admire them or sketch them from life, resulting in the lavishly illustrated *Natural History of the Two Elephants of the Museum.*

though she has probably already been impregnated.

The gestation period is up to twenty-two months. A cow about to give birth moves away from the group and is protected by female attendants that help evacuate the placenta and guard against would-be predators. Twin births are rare. A newborn calf weighs about 100 kilos. It spends its long and carefree childhood playing, taking baths and learning. The only potential dangers awaiting it are the death of its mother or, worse, the breakup of the family unit, which places the calf at the mercy of any large predator and threatens it with death from hunger and thirst.

Family units and herds: a restrictive but advantageous social structure

Whether Asian or African, elephants are remarkably well protected by their social organization. The family unit, which usually numbers no more than ten individuals, blindly follows its leader, the matriarch,

P articular attention was given to the abiding love between the 'spouses', the profusion of caresses prior to copulation, the peculiarities of calving (the mother gives birth standing up), suckling and the countless displays of love and affection showered on their newborn calf. But nothing commanded more admiration than the seemingly virtuous attitude of the father toward his 'wife' and offspring. Actually, this behaviour is seldom observed in the wild, where the bull elephant's interest in his mate and offspring quickly fades.

a senior female whose authority is undisputed. If she charges, or turns and flees, they follow suit. If she is incapacitated, her companions are helpless, immediately at increased risk of dispersal or death.

Within the family unit elephants offer mutual aid, show affection and care for the injured and ailing by means of trunk caresses and a wide range of vocalizations, gestures and mimicry. The family unit is also where irreplaceable life experience – knowledge of migratory trails, water holes, principal dangers – is passed on to others.

In addition to this particularly cohesive structure, groups of six to eight males ten to twelve years of age will leave the group to form separate bachelor herds, engage in friendly sparring among themselves and establish a loose hierarchy. Banished by the mature females, these young bulls often stay on the periphery and play with calves. Large bulls twenty-five and over seldom form clusters of more than two or three individuals. Huge patriarchs – for an elephant never stops growing – often end up living alone or escorted by a lone bull in the prime of life.

Herds and family units often joyously convene at water holes, where they feast on succulent vegetation and indulge in the pleasures of immersion, showers and mud baths. Reunions between close relatives are

In this painting by Charles-Emile Tournemine, a massive, powerful herd of elephants is silhouetted against a sweeping expanse of sky and set off above and below by two sparse groups of birds, one in the air, the other in the water. The animals are accurately depicted. In the foreground we see a large family unit of six or seven cows, plus calves and probably one or two mature bulls that have temporarily joined the group. In the middle ground, to the right, members of another family unit (or else a cluster of banished immature bulls) are careful to keep to the periphery. Collectively they form an African herd that has come to feed peacefully on the soft lakeside vegetation and indulge in the communal pleasure of bathing.

especially affectionate, as when a female
accompanied by her younger sisters greets
the family unit of her mature sisters led
by their aged mother. Elephants can also
congregate by the score, if not by the
hundreds and graze together at specific,
easily located foraging spots. These they
peacefully share with most animals – the
only exceptions are lions and tigers, which
are ruthlessly chased away.

An elephant's appetite

The African elephant consumes an
estimated 200 kilos of vegetation daily in
at least six feeding bouts. Captive
individuals in zoos seldom eat more than
100 kilos a day, but theirs is an
'improved' diet of fruits and vegetables. Working
elephants in Asia generally receive 200 kilos of fodder,
plus titbits.

A wild elephant digests barely half of the rough
forage it devours; between 44 and 48 per cent ends up
as waste. It thus performs an invaluable service, for its
copious, fertile droppings disperse and germinate seeds,
thereby regenerating many plant species. But there is
also the potential drawback of overgrazing, especially

Despite their extreme
caution, elephants
can find themselves in
distress. To rescue one
of her trapped offspring,
a mother will risk either
meeting the same fate
herself or having her
weight cause part of the
cliff to collapse, hurtling
her down a ravine to her
death.

since an elephant can despoil and ransack more than it eats. As it plods through an Asian rice paddy or a gourd or cotton field in Africa, it can do terrible damage, leaving a trail of mangled, trampled crops in its wake. In open woodland or the savanna, herds will topple entire trees to get at foliage or fruit, or else strip them of bark, break branches and gouge trunks, leaving them lifeless and creating wastelands against a backdrop of parched, trodden earth.

In addition to their huge food requirements, elephants need to drink about 1.89 litres of water a day. This accounts for both seasonal migrations in search of food and susceptibility to unexpected climatic changes.

They also require many mineral salts not always found in vegetation: hence the salt licks that they have

These captive Asian elephants are in the process of satisfying their huge appetite. Browsing for high branches and leaves is clearly illustrated and one 'climber' is even shown making use of both its trunk and feet. Apparently the cows have no objection to being approached by the man and child.

Fig. 3.

ploughed up for generations, creating continuously worked mines or quarries with shafts that can be as deep as 4 metres.

The vulnerable elephant's longevity is largely due to the solicitous protection of its kin

The elephant has long been looked upon as 'impregnable' (to quote one 2nd-century rhetorician) and subject to no predators save humans. Of course, this view needs to be qualified. Even a healthy, strapping bull of between twenty-five and forty-five can fall victim to other animals. Poisonous snakes, such as the king cobra, have been known to bite elephants on the trunk. An elephant might be killed if met by an irascible rhinoceros or buffalo that finds itself

Their six meals will be supplemented by fruit or treats. In the wild, some key elements would have to be added: delectable trees uprooted, trunks gouged to the core by tusks, the sun-baked desolation of open woodland that has been overgrazed.

compelled to fight, as they once were in the arenas of ancient Rome. A crocodile in southwestern Sudan was once seen mauling an elephant's trunk so severely that it quickly bled to death.

We should also bear in mind that mature elephants separated from the group run the risk of being set upon by big cats; when lions or tigers are left with no alternative to fighting back they stand their ground with a desperate ferocity that can result in the death of the elephant. Finally, packs of hyenas or wild dogs have been known to chase down lone elephants. In any event, even dominant males, protected by the respect or fear they inspire, seldom stray very far from the family unit or herd, which stands ready to intervene and drive back even the boldest of predators.

A dominant bull may owe its very existence to a

Mature female Asian elephants and their retinue of large bulls will mount spontaneous charges against tigers and the mere sight of this unstoppable steamroller will cause tigers to turn and flee. Mature Asian elephants, especially tusked bulls, jump at the chance to impale cats, though if they are too young or unaccustomed to the presence of tigers, tame elephants may themselves back down.

moment when – during its years as a calf – its mother managed to kill a crocodile or fend off a tiger in the nick of time. In 1950 it was estimated that 25 per cent of all elephant calves in Burma were killed by tigers. African lions, too, are skilled at picking off calves that have lost their mothers to poachers; it is conceivable that mature elephants' aversion to, if not outright fear of, big cats is rooted in a dread harboured throughout their childhood and adolescence. Family units cannot abide the presence of lions (or tigers) and

The elaborate repertory of Indian legends includes stories of elephant calves and the crocodiles that lie in wait for them. In fact, a crocodile may indeed be able to attack (and kill) a young elephant.

herds even less so. As soon as they spot the big cat or cats, the mature cows, often accompanied by several bulls, mount a charge. Generally, the cats will back down and there is no need to press the charge home. In short, an elephant's tremendous strength lies in the fact that it is increased tenfold by the companions in its family unit.

A peaceable colossus confronts human beings

Its potential encounters with predators account for the precautions an elephant takes, its distrust of the unfamiliar and its compelling need to stay within the group, where its elders pass on long years of experience.

This diffidence may have its roots in the distant past. Young mammoths fell victim to mighty *Machairodus*, the sabre-toothed tiger that once roamed Europe. But in Predmost, Moravia, remains of nine hundred to a thousand woolly mammoths were discovered over a hundred years ago, their bones stored more or less systematically and often broken open to draw out the marrow: the work of people, already terrifying predators. Indeed, it has even been suggested that, sparse though human population was in Palaeolithic times, it was as much because of human predation as climatic warming that woolly mammoths gradually headed northeast, only to be trapped by the encroaching forest and the summer flooding of their grazing grounds in the tundra.

In more recent times humans brought their influence to bear in various ways: setting brushfires, permitting grazing or overgrazing by livestock, clearing land for crops and damming rivers, tapping water holes and setting up irrigation systems with the resulting loss or restriction of water in the area – an intolerable situation for heavy water users like elephants. In other respects, however, in different regions and times, widely divergent types of contact emerged between these two species which, for all their obvious differences, have felt drawn to each other by a sense of communality and, at times, mutual curiosity.

Before photography came into its own, many newspapers counted on their resourceful artists to re-create the events deemed most likely to hold readers' attention. Since they could not cover a story on the spot or receive wire photos (which did not come into general use until 1928, in *The Scotsman*), newspapers used illustrations based on the sometimes fanciful details that someone telegraphed them, along with a smattering of geography that served as a springboard for the artist's imagination. Here, in a scene reminiscent of a buffalo stampede in the American West, an elephant herd – the size of the ears and the sheer number of animals suggest Africa rather than Asia – has not only brought a train to a standstill but knocked it off the tracks. This bloodless exoticism may have been intended to underscore the power of these animals as they stood up to the unremitting advance of human technology. Nowadays, some might interpret the scene the other way around: 'nuisance' animals beating a quick retreat before the inconvenienced people.

Asia and its elephants lived together as partners for thousands of years. There they were treasured, deified and venerated as noble champions, hunting companions and loving friends. In Africa, however, although the elephant commanded respect – it was seen as the father or chief of animals – when it came into contact with civilization, the result was violence and death.

CHAPTER 2

ASIA AND AFRICA: A TWO-SIDED PICTURE

Akbar (1542–1605) consolidated and greatly expanded the Mogul empire his grandfather Babur had founded. Elephants were accorded a place of honour in his palaces (left). Allegory of Africa (right), from a Sicilian mural.

Why this difference in attitude? Why Asia and not Africa?

Despite claims to the contrary, African elephants can be fully tamed, especially when young. Even a mature wild elephant can get used to inquisitive researchers or gawking tourists and can tell them apart from poachers or culling teams. They can also be trained: Leopold II, the king of Belgium, successfully put them to work in what is now Zaire in the late 19th century. They are capable of bonding and they chase down lions the way their Asian kin do tigers. If they come across as less 'intelligent', it is due simply to the comparison people make with Asian elephants, which are superbly trained and coached by handlers who can draw on procedures dating back thousands of years. Their spontaneous 'anthropophilia' is more elusive than that attributed to the ancestral dog or the dolphin, but their curiosity about people, which is initially friendly, is well established.

That animals – including elephants – and nature figure prominently in Brahmanic and Buddhist civilizations is obvious but inconclusive. Why these civilizations and not, say, Judeo-Christian ones?

African religions, however, which are also deeply rooted in the world of nature and animals, are less sympathetic towards the elephant than they are towards a number of other animals. The domestication of

Coastal India was fairly well charted by 1517, twenty years after the arrival of Vasco da Gama; the Indo-Gangetic plain and the roughly north-to-south course of the Indus River were already known, thanks to ancient traditions and medieval travellers. This map from 1519 reveals gaps in knowledge (errors in proportion) and aspects of India Europeans found most intriguing: fortified towns, clusters of tiny islands, exotic warriors and large, heavy animals, including the rhinoceros and the elephant.

indigenous elephants in Africa was largely confined to the Maghreb (northwestern Africa) and the outer reaches of Nubia and Ethiopia and probably declined when elephants became scarce or disappeared from those regions many years ago.

What part could the elephant have played in Africa?

Forest-dwelling tribes in black Africa, especially wherever tsetse flies were rampant, had little opportunity to supplement their diet with protein; for them, the elephant was seen as a mountain of meat to be hunted and killed. However, in savanna regions that sheltered hoofed mammals or supported limited raising of livestock – thus, where natives ate a considerable amount of meat (witness the Masai) – there was little point in adding dangerous elephant hunts to the already gruelling task of hunting lions, panthers and other animals that prey on people and livestock.

Human population was often sparse and elephants lived an unrestricted, self-regulating existence within an environment that humans did not alter in any major way. Brushfires, for example, simply

B edecked in muslin, fine cotton and jewelry, this Indian noblewoman is out for a ride amongst the flowers, holding one of her favourite animals and mounted on another. The big bull elephant's slender tusks have not been sawed off or ornamented. Its matching 'outfit' consists of a headband, a wide, flat saddle with a back and cushions and a neck girth which, among other things, secures the huge protective saddlecloth draped over its back. There are no stirrups. The noblewoman must climb on to her mount while it is kneeling. Although the uplifted trunk suggests a greeting, chances are the elephant is asking for a treat.

shifted animals from one area to another. Elephants kept their distance, seldom ravaged what little cropland there was, and set upon livestock even less and the people respected their strength, wisdom and benevolence – not to mention their daunting power. It would have taken a material change in their way of thinking to hit upon the idea of attempting to forge a close bond with an elephant. How would a person have come by one that was 'ready, willing and able' to serve? And, in any case, what would have been the purpose? Elephants could not very well have been used in epic battles, or as working animals enlisted to clear paths and trails (which materialized naturally in the savanna), till fields (which could be ploughed by oxen) or fell trees (a job which, in the end, could be done more effectively with fire and patience). Last but not least, bush elephants are difficult to tame fully; in circuses and modern zoos, handlers are especially wary of sudden changes in mood and onsets of musth in even the most submissive of females.

Obviously, these explanations are far from complete, but they are not mere simplifications.

T his allegory of Africa (above left) features dark-skinned people shielding themselves from the sun. Neither the precipitous mountains in the background nor the diminutive, piglet-like creatures – so unlike the as-yet-undiscovered bush elephant – can disguise the allusions to the east coast from Ethiopia to Zanzibar (costumes, servants, slaves). A liberal dose of imagination makes this a classic example of exoticism.

Elephants and their place in the civilizations of lush, densely populated, monsoon-swept Asia

From India to China humans found themselves in close proximity to indigenous fauna and the elephant's

strength and sagacity earned it a place as a chief or deity. However, perhaps the elephant's relationship with the tiger – even more aggressive and fearsome than the African lion – added to people's respect for it; the elephant is the only animal with the reassuring ability to put tigers to flight and kill them, or assist in hunting them by tracking them down and manoeuvring them towards hunters. Tigers' natural fear of elephants is a recurrent theme in the earliest Sanskrit epics.

It is also possible that the might of this noble beast was recognized and sought after as much for warfare as for hunting. Elephants could prove advantageous if trained to act in concert with the horses the Indo-Europeans had introduced; they could take part in battles involving large, concentrated complements of soldiers, which were easy to attack and trample. Here again, human population density was a factor and, in the case of the Kshatriyas (Aryan warriors), proved as influential as the war horse and the hunting dog.

Tamed and domesticated over five thousand years ago, elephants still play a fundamental part in the two religions India bequeathed to the world. Brahmanism and Buddhism regard them as not only the strongest animals in all creation, but the wisest, as well.

According to one hypothesis, elephants were initially pressed into service for 'noble' duties: warfare, tiger hunts and the unrivalled prestige of being the mount of chiefs. As in North Africa, Egypt and the Greco-Roman world – all of which were, after all, influenced by India – a great many illustrations and most Sanskrit texts cast elephants almost exclusively in a military role and generally depict them with 'mada-moistened temples', that is, in a state of heightened aggressiveness.

Another school of thought is based on the Indus valley civilizations of Mohenjo Daro and Harappa (in today's Pakistan), which flourished a thousand years before the arrival of Indo-European warriors to the region. There, this docile beast with the strength of sixty men may have been called upon to help out with heavy tasks, even though it has only three times the load-bearing capacity of camels (which are incomparably less expensive), seldom works more than six hours a day and requires substantial amounts of food, up-keep and care.

These huge stone figures eternally stand guard over the approach to the Ming tombs near Beijing.

Elephants are known to have been tamed for transportation and military purposes in China as far back as the 2nd millennium BC. They were in continuous use throughout the Ming (1368–1644) and Manchu (1644–1911) dynasties. The spread and triumph of Buddhism, dating back to the dawn of the Christian era, enhanced the standing and symbolism of this noble, powerful and wise animal that was said to have fathered Sakyamuni, the last known reincarnation of the Buddha. Buddha riding an elephant (opposite).

Whatever the purpose of domesticating elephants may have been at first, their increasingly stronger ties with humans fostered greater intimacy on both sides. In all available information about elephants in Burma, Laos, Thailand, Cambodia, Vietnam and even China, there is as much emphasis on their role in warfare as there is on the powerful influence of Indian culture. Therefore, despite the concepts of gentleness, reverence for all life, metempsychosis (the passing of a soul at death into another body, human or animal) and zoophilia that India passed on to civilizations farther east, plenty of wild animals, including tigers and elephants, were killed in those regions, too, not to mention the toll wars and other clashes – far bloodier than those in Africa – took on human life.

We cannot help concluding that there is no single, all-encompassing explanation for the different treatment of elephants in Asia and Africa. We are still a long way from conclusively accounting for the fact that, since the dawn of time, Asia preferred its elephants alive and Africa, dead.

Mother Asia

The earliest Indian civilizations to be documented in any detail

flourished in the Indus valley between Harappa and Mohenjo Daro, from 2500 to 1700 BC. By this point, the elephant already figured prominently as sign, symbol and totem. The animal was depicted on steatite seals with a long piece of cloth draped over its back – thus, domesticated even then – and its use as a mount and war animal was widely documented in the 2nd millennium BC. Numerous texts derived from oral tradition were disseminated by the gradual but massive influx of Indo-Iranians (Aryans) around the 16th century BC. These nomadic, livestock-raising invaders from the steppes, who brought with them the saddle horse and the mighty battle-axe, overwhelmed the subcontinent, sweeping over northwestern India and most of the Gangetic plain, pushing southwards towards the Deccan and then turning north to the valleys of the Himalayas. Wherever they went, they found elephants and firmly rooted traditions involving their capture, training, military usefulness, noble attributes and faithfulness. The earliest Hindu sacred writings (including the most ancient of all the Vedas, the *Rig-Veda*) allude to the Aryans' familiarity with this wild yet tractable beast and it was very quickly incorporated into their religion and everyday life.

The elephant's place in the Hindu pantheon

Elephants crop up at every level of the elaborate and teeming Hindu pantheon, which is centred around the famous trinity of Brahma, Vishnu and Siva. The elephant Airavata, mount of Indra, god of rain, thunder and warfare, was believed to have been the first to emerge from Brahma's eggshell. Two elephants, with the evocative names Mahapadma ('great forest') and Saumanasa ('keeper of soma', the sacred juice), were the massive pillars of the world and bore the earth on their enormous heads. Ganesh, second son of Parvati and Siva and chief of the *ganas* (demigods that do

Chandragupta (313–289 BC) was the founder of the Maurya dynasty in India. The mainstay of his military might was the war elephant, which he emblazoned on his coins. He provided five hundred elephants that swung the Battle of Ipsus (301 BC) in favour of the coalition against Antigonus I.

The numerous, often divergent, legends of Indian mythology revolve around its chief deities. The elephant-headed god seldom enjoyed supreme status, unlike Indra, who can be seen mounted on his elephant (opposite, above) on the cloud on the upper left, which is about to yield its contents at his command.

Siva's bidding), is still one of the best-loved of all Indian deities; he is typically depicted as an elephant-headed god mounted on a rat, with a handsome trunk and a single, sometimes broken, tusk. As the Remover of Obstacles and Lord of Beginnings, he is invoked at the start of any undertaking, be it commercial, intellectual, literary or scholastic. In the past many manuscripts opened with the words 'Honour to Lord Ganesh'; modern authors do the same to this day. References to his friendliness, benevolence and prudence date from the middle of the 1st millennium BC and during certain periods (notably the Middle Ages) he was hailed as the greatest of all the gods. Today his knowledge and perception are thought to bring good fortune to students preparing for their exams.

Supreme Vedic deity Indra (below), intoxicated by soma and bristling with weaponry, hurls thunderbolts, wins battles and causes celestial cows (clouds) to release their milk for the greater good of the peasants. A hearty eater and fabled tippler, quick-tempered and rakish but also munificent and friendly, he epitomizes the Aryan warrior chief. In classic Brahmanism (the first phase of Hinduism), Indra is simply the chief of the terrestrial demigods known as demons. His charger is not a horse, but Airavata, the mighty elephant born of the churning of the primordial sea of milk.

One of Indra's emblems is the *ankus*, or elephant goad, seen here in his first left hand.

Queen Sirimahamaya, impregnated by Indra's sacred elephant

Buddhism is thought to have emerged within a warrior

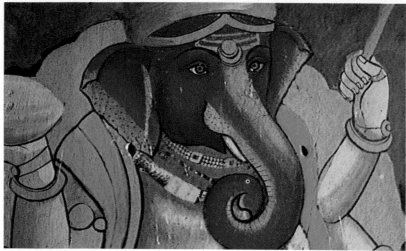

family from the kingdom of Magadha, in a minimally Aryanized region around the town of Kapilavastu in today's Nepal. But during its expansion into India, it underwent significant changes and absorbed countless miraculous details harking back to Vedic deities and themes. This was particularly true of elephants, which originally were less Aryan than horses or livestock.

In his penultimate reincarnation, the future Buddha was Vessantara, son of a mighty king who derived his omnipotence from a miraculous elephant that granted his every wish. (The last great temptation this prefiguration of Christ had to face came in the form of a demon, Indra, mounted on the elephant Airavata.) His reincarnation as Gautama or Sakyamuni – the historical Buddha – occurred inside the body of an undefiled virgin who was impregnated, not by the dove of the Holy Spirit, but by the trunk of an elephant.

Queen Sirimahamaya was the most beautiful of all women – 'her arms more lithesome than an elephant's trunk, her legs and thighs more slender' – and devoted her life to fasting, austerity and chastity. One summer night by the light of the full moon, she dreamed she was transported to a magnificent palace on top of the

This miniature fairly glows with the gentle, easygoing disposition of Ganesh, the elephant-headed god. Needless to say, he is strong. One of his tusks is missing, making the diminutive survivor all the more powerful. But this deity is never aggressive. An elaborate symbolism casts him in the role of Lord of Beginnings, Undertakings and Examinations. He was also a welcome addition to Buddhist legend.

Here Ganesh (opposite above) is seen with Queen Sirimahamaya, mother of the future Buddha – a meeting not unlike the Visitation or the Annunciation.

Himalayas. 'A silvery-white elephant descended from the mountains, entered my room and bowed down before me. In its trunk it bore a lotus. I was awakened by the call of a bird.' The chaste and comely queen painlessly gave birth to the fruit of the divine elephant's trunk-phallus beneath a tree in the tranquillity of the Lumbini Garden.

Naturally, elephants figure prominently in picture versions of Buddhist stories. When Buddhism moved out of India and into vast neighbouring lands – including China, where elephants were tamed as far back as the Yin dynasty (1750–1123 BC) – it took these elephant themes and myths with it.

In the realm of the white elephant

The extremely rare white elephant (which is actually light grey with glints of silver) commanded the very highest respect in Buddhist-dominated areas of western Indochina, where, until recently,

Siam, Laos and Burma venerated the extremely rare white elephant, which recalled the conception of Buddha. Escorted back to court with the utmost deference, it would lead a long, sheltered life amid finery and the distinction of opened parasols.

large numbers of wild elephants still roamed. A white elephant graced the centre of the flag of ancient Siam (Thailand). It was also venerated in Laos and Burma. In the course of his many animal reincarnations, the Enlightened One entered the body of not just the wisest of beasts, but the rarest and most handsome specimen of them all: 'Mouth open, head the colour of cochineal, tusks gleaming like silver, all aglitter with precious stones, clad in the finest of golden tulle, his limbs and organs were flawlessly proportioned, his bearing majestic.'

Whenever a white elephant was spotted in the forest, it was captured with the utmost care, ministered to by a host of attendants and adorned with exquisite jewelry. It was served luscious delicacies in the hope of prolonging its life and with any luck it lived to a ripe old age. Its death prompted consternation, grief and fear, from the king down to his humblest subject. A replacement had to be quickly found.

Occasionally one of these revered elephants might be trained to carry out death sentences and crush the head of a condemned man beneath one of its feet – a practice reported as recently as the late 19th century. But it was not considered to be absolutely necessary for an elephant executioner to be white and sacred in order to dispense divine justice.

War elephants

We do not know if the domestication of elephants came about as a result of their military use. At any rate, the army of the Vedas consisted of four elements: elephants, cavalry, chariots and infantry. The basic fighting unit, or *patti*, grouped one elephant, one chariot, three horses and five foot soldiers. An *akshanhini* (massed army) numbered 21,870 elephants, an equivalent complement of chariots, 65,610 horses and 109,350 troops – 21,870 *patti* in all! A typical battle formation deployed 45 elephants, 45 chariots, 220 horses and 675 infantrymen. The elephants were the first to charge, throwing enemy ranks into disorder.

Persia's Homer, the great poet Firdawsi (born 10th century) wrote the *Shah-nameh*, an epic chronicle of his native Persia until the conversion of Khorasan to Islam. The 17th-century miniature on the right depicts a battle between the Persians and the Turks.

There are more reports of elephants carrying out death sentences than actual illustrations of them cast in this unexpected role. A particularly long and difficult training period must have been required to coax this naturally gentle creature into calmly crushing a human head on the executioner's block.

In his history of the Mogul emperor Akbar, Abufazl recounted how around 1567 'most of the great lords of India had come to bow down and kiss the ground, except Rana [Prince] Uday-Singh.... He was proud of his steep mountains and impregnable fortresses.' Akbar could not allow these acts of defiance to rally pious Hindus against the Muslim conquerors. Uday-Singh's fortress, Chitor, surrendered, but only after a terrible siege. However, one of the rana's supporter's, Rai Surjan, was still in control of the fortified town of Ranthambhor, pictured here. The attack began on 10 January 1569. Huge cannons, mortars and culverins were reportedly brought in by thousands of oxen and deployed on level terrain by thousands of men under constant pounding by Rajput (Hindu) artillery. An advance from covered trenches forced Rai Surjan to capitulate on 19 March. Akbar's elephants peacefully lumbered into town, which was spared the carnage – including an onslaught of three hundred elephants – that Chitor had endured.

As they did so, they knocked down stockades and battlements. A single enraged elephant was reckoned to be the equal of 6000 horses. Others were pressed into service as pack animals or as mobile bridges over deep fords. Each elephant and its crew – the handler and two or three additional men on its back, a protective detail of soldiers and noncombatants bringing up the rear – formed a self-contained unit.

War elephants were given special training and care inside pens, where they could be regularly monitored and inspected. Of prime importance was their ability to respond to commands and attack (sometimes under the intoxicating influence of arrack, an alcoholic drink made from fermented rice) without breaking formation. They wore protective leather armour, while a quiver on the saddle housed the spears and arrows that the soldiers on their backs rained down on the enemy.

Champion elephants

Armoured elephants were generally deployed in the frequent wars that erupted between princes and rajas. Battles usually began with an individual duel between two huge bulls amid intertwined trunks and the clash of ivory.

There is probably a connection between the ferocity (and, in a sense, the beauty) of these bouts and the annual 'championship matches' which, according to Roman author Aelian (2nd century), were already being held in India in times of peace. To avert a deadly outcome for either champion, if not both, a low wall was introduced to separate the contestants in these bouts and prevent the winner from finishing off the loser. Occasionally, tusks would be strengthened by sawing off the tips; this practice also resulted in fewer fatal wounds. A footnote: when two elephants in musth confronted each other, the first victims might very well have been their respective mahouts or handlers.

Now and again, these matches involved more than two contestants. Wild elephants were forced into a clearly demarcated ring to challenge tame champions –

A lead female has just stumbled and cannot get back up despite her mahout's exhortations. The soldiers are trying to give her assistance by pushing the wheels of a heavy cannon, which might get bogged down on the rugged slope. The Second Afghan War (1879–80) was particularly gruelling. After the British missionaries at Kabul were massacred, counterattacking forces under General (later Earl) Frederick Sleigh Roberts had to withdraw from Peshawar and cross the Hindu Kush through the lofty Khyber Pass, where in 1842 another British army had tragically been wiped out.

a variation on a hunting technique that makes use of tame elephants to drive herds of their wild kin into the open. This seldom led to violent, all-out clashes. The wild animals, realizing that the odds were against them, turned tail instead of fighting back; their big but tuskless matriarchs were no match for huge, overfed, highly trained domesticated elephants.

During championship bouts, elephants collided head on, intertwined trunks and tried to kill each other's mahout, who ran the greatest risk of all.

By and large, hunting with elephants was a prerogative of royalty and power, for this dangerous diversion was something only people of considerable means could afford. The quarry might be buffalo or gaur (wild cattle), which, even when enraged and charging, posed little danger to men perched on virtually unassailable mounts. By hunting leopards and especially tigers, noblemen could not only fulfil their duty to safeguard peasants and livestock, but display their courage and indulge in the heightened pleasure of a potentially hazardous sport as well.

Everything was part of a carefully orchestrated plan. Dogs fearlessly roused the tigers, which beat a retreat as the elephants approached. Handlers manoeuvred the elephants in from all sides, blocking the cats' escape routes and making it easier for the mounted hunters to gun them down. Discipline was

War elephants in the service of the Mogul emperor Akbar (above). His stables are said to have housed six thousand of these giants and he reportedly crossed the Ganges to conquer Bengal with six hundred 'crack' elephants.

A white hunter opens fire in relative safety. Another loaded rifle is kept at the ready if his first shots miss. The tiger backs down and the bull elephant will finish off the cat if it is only wounded.

crucial: undertrained elephants might turn and flee and overtrained ones might charge too soon. Therefore, this form of hunting was not entirely risk-free, particularly if a tiger, once hemmed in by the elephants, was able to hide in tall grass. From there it might strike at the nearest elephant, perhaps at the trunk but especially at the tail or back, where it might find a more succulent spot into which to sink its teeth; its chances would be improved if the handler and hunters held their fire for fear of shooting one another.

The pageantry and prestige of elephants

In general, elephants came to embody royalty because of the unusually high price they commanded, the expense their training and daily upkeep incurred and their potential usefulness in warfare and hunting. Meticulously groomed and harnessed to the raja's (or his guests') palanquin, they were used as much for ceremonial processions and journeys as for anything else. Owning and displaying saddle elephants – gorgeously decked out in rich cloth

M obile lovemaking, Venetian-style, was one of the pleasures of owning this prestigious mount, although the ride might prove rougher than in a gondola.

and tooled leather and adorned with gold and silver jewelry set off by pearls, precious stones, feathers and tinkling bells that heralded their approach – came to be regarded as an important measure of prestige. Even the mahout's hooked driving goad, the *ankus*, might well be made of gold and rubies, like the one Kipling described in his *Second Jungle Book*.

Moreover, if we credit 4th-century Macedonian general Nearchus' description of India, a fine specimen might be one of the many gifts a suitor offered his beloved.

The elephant as draft animal and beast of burden

No sooner were elephants pressed into service as mounts than they found themselves carrying loads – chiefly military gear and provisions – or hauling vehicles and artillery. Along with his war elephants, 14th-century Turkic conqueror Timur is said to have deployed a permanent contingent of ninety-five elephants to help build the mosque at Samarkand. The Japanese used them as pack animals in Burma during the Second World War, as did the

In Asia elephants are used for clearing woodland and working in marshes. An elephant fells a tree by pushing it over with the concentrated strength of its forehead or upper trunk and, if need be, by shifting all its weight to the forefeet for additional leverage. Once a tree has been uprooted, its branches are lopped off and the timber is cut up into logs, which the elephant picks up with its trunk or lifts on to its tusks for transport. The heaviest tree trunks are dragged to a river or loading dock. Judging by its unusually long tusks, the elephant in the foreground is not only well advanced in years but highly experienced and remarkably strong. The elephants working in unison under the direction of one mahout appear to be much younger.

Viet Cong in Vietnam. Elephants are still used in Southeast Asia wherever Caterpillar bulldozers, much less wheeled vehicles, cannot negotiate muddy or otherwise impassable terrain and they can still be found hauling and performing such heavy-duty tasks as felling trees, carrying out logs and clearing paths or roads. When an elephant pushes with its forehead (thus concentrating all its strength on a limited surface) and braces itself with its feet (which can spontaneously locate and improve on the best anchor points), it is in most cases as powerful as a big, fixed-bed, broader-'browed' bulldozer, if not more so. Strong, gentle, docile females are suitable for most tasks; but bulls are better at hauling logs, which they lift on to their tusks and hold securely in place with their trunk.

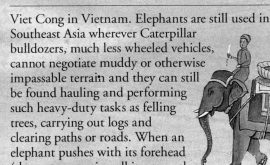

An elephant has scarcely more than three times the load-bearing capacity of a camel, but it can usually be harnessed and made to pull a far heavier burden. The animal is hitched to the vehicle in tow by a wide piece of material that follows the curvature of its back and is secured over a saddlecloth by two shoulder girths. Judging by its size, the individual pictured here is a young bull in training.

Elephant castes

As with horses, elephants were probably used primarily as mounts, not as draft animals. It is significant that in Sanskrit literature elephants were already being differentiated not only according to age, behaviour, provenance and smell, but by occupation (warfare, pageantry, riding), disposition (tractable, 'rogue') and breed. There were eight breeds in all: Kalingas, Bengalis and those associated with Brahma's earth-bearing pillars were considered the finest.

There was also the criterion of caste. In the late 19th century elephant dealers marketed animals that ranged in class from Koomeriah down to Dwasala and Meergs. Koomeriahs were the standard of perfection and as such connoted royalty: broad, burly body; short, colossal limbs (especially the hind legs); a straight, flat back that sloped from shoulder to tail; high forehead; massive head and chest; short, thick neck; a trunk that was wide at the base and thickened by a prominent swelling between the eyes; and a shaggy tail that was long but did not touch the ground. They stood at least 2.75 metres tall. On the whole, their gentle, docile, fearless temperament was superior to that of other elephants. In the 1880s an animal of this calibre might fetch upward of $10,000 at a time when the average elephant cost about $750 and a decent cow about $1000.

Care and breaking-in

The *Hastividyarnava*, the age-old handbook for elephant tamers, spells out prescribed procedures in minute detail and is still in use today. As far back as eighteen hundred years ago, Aelian described how wounds were healed with hot water and butter salves, inflammations treated with warm, blood-red deer meat, ophthalmia with cow's milk and other diseases with red wine. We shall dispense with the particulars of elephant care and focus instead on the process that turns a wild elephant into a tame one.

Although force is occasionally needed to break in

An elephant used for work or transportation will often forge an indissoluble bond with its mahout. In general, an elephant understands what its mahout wants by touch alone. Occasionally, the handler may give his

mount's sensitive ears a sharp jab with the driving goad, but only for manoeuvres an elephant would ordinarily refuse to carry out. This hooked implement is less commonly used to punish an act of disobedience or to subdue a rogue elephant. At any rate, mature elephants, even tame ones, are chained at night as a precautionary measure. An unexpected onset of musth might create a serious disturbance and a successful escape would cost its owner dearly.

so-called rogue elephants, in virtually all cases the first requisite step is to win the animal's confidence, affection and gratitude. The German philosopher Albertus Magnus (*c.* 1200–80) described the procedure as recounted by Avicenna (980–1037) and his Indian sources. A 'mean' man would beat the trainee elephant in the pit in which it had been trapped; a 'nice' man, with whom the wretched beast eventually bonded, chased the first man away.

A wild bull elephant has been captured and securely lashed to a tree. Akbar, who has come personally to inspect it, is accompanied by many servants, as well as tame elephants to lead the newcomer away for training, if need be.

Chasse Pour Pre

on fait une estacade ou palissade de gros pieux ou arbres entiers dont l'enceinte e[t]
laisse la baze de ce triangle ouuert pour la fermer quand on veut, on a des pieux tous p[ ]
de plusieurs milliers d'hommes a quelques lieues de cette palissade, ils font un grand ce[ ]
font fuir les elephans sauuages, les conduisants uers l'estacade ou les ayant reduits (j[ ]
on a une porte a l'endroit le plus estroit et l'on y fait entrer un elephant docile qui ua [ ]
[ ]eint l'elephant domestique ou les fait sortir de cette enceinte et l'on les laisse ainsi [ ]

Les Elephans,

ire et a quelque fois une a deux lieux détour ou de circuit on
e, Vis a vis de cette enceinte on fait dans la forest une battüe,
es tambours des trompetes et des mousquets ils époumantent et,
nent auec les pieux preparez et pour les prendre et les ... ouser
le premier Elephant sauuage auquel on jette une corde au col et son
quils soient accoutumez

'A Hunt to Capture Elephants'

The elephants depicted in the following series of 18th-century watercolours belonged to the king of Siam (Thailand). The accompanying captions make for fascinating reading.

"A corral or stockade is fashioned from large stakes or entire trees, forming a triangular enclosure that is sometimes one or two leagues around.... A shelter for several thousand men is built in the forest a few leagues from this stockade. They fan out into a huge circle and with drums, trumpets and muskets they terrify the wild elephants and put them to flight, all the while driving them towards the stockade, where, after breaking them in, they confine them with stakes specially designed for capturing and taming them. There is a gate at the narrowest point and a docile elephant is led in to distract the first wild elephant so that it may be roped and tied to it. The [captives] are thus led out of the enclosure and so remain until they have been tamed."

Escuries des Uleph

Baque Elephant a son escurie particuliere bastie ou de brique ou de bamboux et plusieurs
x un baston aubout duquel il y a Comme a un Croc de batelier Une pointe auec Une
nt ala Campagne assez loin et reuiennent le Soir charger de grandes herbes pour
Riues entieres en tour deson palais qui ne Sont composées que de maisons pour les e
r fait Cuire d'un sorte de grain Comme des Lentilles on y met du poivre *long* dedans qui
on appelle Poivre d'elephant on met ce grain en boules arosses Comme la teste d'un e

'Elephant Stables and Feeding'

"Every elephant has its own stable of brick or bamboo and several attendants; the man who controls the elephant is called a mahout. He carries a staff and at the end of it there is a kind of boathook with two sharp points – one straight, the other curved – which he uses to jab the elephant's brow. The other men go rather a long way off into the forest and return in the evening with tall grass for the elephants. The king of Siam has a great many elephants. There are entire streets around his palace that are lined with nothing but houses for elephants and each one has a large entrance with double doors. A kind of cereal, not unlike lentils, is cooked for them. To this is added a variety of long pepper that is black, a half-finger in length and rough-skinned: it is called elephant pepper. This cereal is shaped into a ball about as big as a child's head and placed inside the elephant's mouth."

et leur manger-

uy le seruent, on appelle Cornac Celuy qui gouuerne l'eleph
ournee dont il pique le front de l'elephant les autres hom
nts Le Roy de Siam a vne grande quantité d'Elephans on
Chacune a vne grande porte Cochere a deux baftans o
t dela longeur dela moitié d'un doigt et tout chagrine
met dans la bouche de l'elephant.

64

combat.

D'un tigre auec des eléphants quelque fois l'on v

Le tigre par le milieu du corps et le jetter en

qui en dessus lui ordonne il le foule auec les

tigre tâche principalement de prendre l

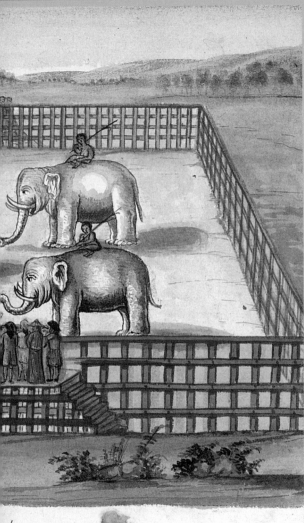

'Fight between a Tiger and Elephants'

"The elephant sometimes wraps its trunk around the middle of the tiger's body and flings it into the air when its handler or rider orders it to do so. It tramples [the tiger] with its feet or gores it with its tusks. The tiger endeavours to sink its claws into the elephant's trunk."

éphant prendre auec sa trompe
iand son cornac ou lhomme
ou le reuoit sur ses dents. le
ype auec ses griffes et lélephan

Since elephants are accustomed to satisfying an enormous appetite, food and drink would be systematically withheld to wear the captive down. It would also be subjected to a continuous barrage of noise, its weakness thus exacerbated by loss of sleep. At this point, the trainee would be ready to be subdued by the large tame elephants that entered the enclosure in which it was kept two or three at a time.

Eventually the trainee would learn to accept food from human hands – a sign that it had fully understood its predicament – would lose its aggressiveness and become fit to be trained. Sometimes a domesticated elephant would be tethered nearby throughout the process to give a trainee confidence and show by example that it can eat proffered food. At every stage, trainers or drivers would act as interpreters or intermediaries between the elephants.

From India to Africa

Asian civilizations undoubtedly influenced a number of African civilizations that harboured or made use of elephants. In Egypt the idea that elephants could be useful, if not indispensable, in time of war came from the East; diminutive elephants from the land of Punt (adjoining Ethiopia) were captured and transported to the Nile delta. Thanks to Asia, Carthaginian elephants were trained for use in military campaigns against Rome and Ethiopia, too, felt its influence by way of the Indian Ocean and the Red Sea. While the area around Aksum in northern Ethiopia remained staunchly Christian, so-called white Africa was quickly converted to Islam during the Damascus and Baghdad caliphates (7th–9th centuries), which were quite familiar with elephants, their handlers and their advantages in times of war and peace.

As Islam spread so did elephants,

The Indian Ocean provided Arab merchants from Oman to Zanzibar with an avenue for the slave trade and the export of ivory to the Far East. Other commodities of less consequence (wild or domestic hides) helped make this business even more lucrative. But the return flow of imports from Asia did not include tame elephants or domestication techniques.

at least to a degree. The hero of the *Thousand and One Nights*, Harun al-Rashid himself, sent Charlemagne an Indian elephant as a gift. Through the Middle Ages Islam was gaining a foothold in part of elephant-rich India and modern Pakistan and Bangladesh; it was also spreading towards black Africa (which it continues to do to this day). Arab sultans from Zanzibar to Oman channelled ivory and slaves to India and the West; but there was no reverse flow of drivers, trainers or tame Indian elephants to teach their wild African kin how to obey and work for human masters. In all probability, transporting white gold on the backs of black slaves seemed more natural and cost-effective than running the risk of using animals that might prove overwhelming and unable to get along with their domesticated Asian cousins.

The fact that, for one reason or another, black Africa ultimately preferred dead elephants to living ones did not prevent it from knowing all about them and observing them alive and in the wild for thousands of years. Elephants provided generous supplies of meat for human consumption; hide for bracelets and armour; hair for necklaces; tusks for war, hunting or signalling horns; and ivory for handicrafts, jewelry and, above all, export. Consequently, civilizations that prized

Certain subspecies of African elephant are known to have been domesticated since ancient times. This has been clearly documented not only in northwestern Africa, but also in Ethiopia and even in Nubia and Sudan. The impeccably harnessed and decorated elephant in this relief carving (below) seems to be keeping a jealous watch over kneeling captives.

living elephants may once have existed in the very heart of Africa. The living elephant is generally regarded as a symbol of longevity, strength, wisdom and justice. Alfred Edmund Brehm, author of an immense 19th-century study of animals, wrote,' "Elephants will leave you alone if you don't bother them," a sheik once told me on the banks of the Blue Nile. "They left my father alone and his father before him. When the monsoon season is nigh, I hang amulets on tall poles; for these righteous animals, that is enough. They revere the word of Allah's prophet! They fear the retribution that awaits blasphemers. They are righteous animals." '

In northern Africa the name of many a Berber water hole, spring, lake or river alludes to the elephants that must have frequented them at one time or another. Carthaginian statesman Hanno reported spotting elephants in the 3rd century BC.

In the interior of Africa the natural and the supernatural are tightly interwoven; plants, animals and rocks are clearly associated with unseen forces both good and evil. Totemism – the belief in a blood tie between a family or clan and a group of animals or plants – forbids, for example, the killing, eating or touching of an animal thought to be sacred. This worked to the elephant's advantage in various tribes, such as the Ndovu among the Bapimbwé of Tanganyika (modern Tanzania). The elephants of the Ruwenzori range (on the Uganda–Zaire border) – the 'Mountains of the Moon' – are among the biggest on earth and likened to the mountains they roam. Materializing from the mist, then fading back into it, they

In Africa elephants were hardly ever regarded as harmful, crop-ravaging animals. More than anything, they – like mammoths before them – were looked upon as mountains of meat. Hunting them with traps and spears was very dangerous and considered a test of manhood. An Angolan statuette in ivory depicts a deity (right).

roam amongst giant flowers, huge nettles and lobelia.

In the folklore of many peoples that cast living animals in a comical light, the elephant ranks above the lion, the hippopotamus and the panther.

The glorified mountain of meat

Certain African tribal customs carry the personification of elephants to fairly considerable lengths. It is believed that after death chiefs and other powerful individuals can turn into or be reincarnated as elephants, usually matriarchs, which should therefore be respected and honoured so that they might permit and abet the killing of members of their family. Even these reincarnations must be placed within a context of death.

In fact, most magic formulas designed to conjure up an elephant's spirit deal in one way or another with

bringing about its death and guarding against its revenge. The Kru people of the Ivory Coast take the flower of the raffia palm (its pistil resembles a tusk) and a mushroom, then mash them together and smear the paste over their bodies. Hunters refrain from sexual contact, and all the villagers dance, often several nights in a row.

However, in Gabon and along the middle Congo, among the Mindassa people of the Ogooué River, magical practices intended to appease the spirits of their future victims are rooted in sexuality. Often led by the village chief, acting as *Nganga djoko,* or 'master of the elephant rite', the ceremony (as documented by Even) is quite elaborate. The day before the deadly hunt, the *Nganga djoko* and his wife retire to their hut and have intercourse. She keeps out of sight while the hunt is in progress but emerges to suck blood from the trunk-phallus that her husband has severed. During the festivities following the elephant's death, the *Nganga djoko* feigns sorrow and sheds tears over the creature that has been slain.

But thorough familiarity with this munificent beast's habits and virtues did little to change the attitudes of black Africa towards it. It was the Asian elephant that, by way of the Mediterranean world, so profoundly influenced Western civilization. The fact that European colonization of the Indian hinterland predated that of the African interior by more than three centuries simply strengthened – until the 19th century – the view that living elephants are our fellow creatures, benevolent friends and strong, considerate helpers.

The Hottentots practised all forms of hunting. No animal was considered more troublesome than the lion, which attacked people and livestock alike. First they wounded their quarry with arrows (usually poisoned), then finished it off at close range with bludgeons or assegais – javelins with broad, razor-sharp iron tips (likewise poisoned). Before it expired, the lion usually had time to pounce on one of the hunters and possibly inflict serious wounds on two or three others. Elephants were hunted in much the same way: they were riddled with arrows. An elephant first had to be separated from the family or herd that would surely come to its defence, just as a lion had to be separated from his lionesses. The slaughter depicted in this European engraving (right) may have been prompted, at least in part, by the demand for ivory.

Tem est bestia elephans nomine. Phisiologus dicit de eo
quoniam intellectum magnum habet in se. Concupiscentiam
uero coitus minime in se habere dicitur. Tempore cum uoluerit
filios procreare. uadit in orientem cum femina sua usque in
proximum paradisi. Est autem ibidem herba mandragora
nomine. de cuius fructu femina prior degustet. Et tunc mas
culum illuc deducet. ut persuasus manducet. Postquam
uero manducauerit ambo conueniunt sibi statimque con
cipit. Cum autem uenerit tempus pariendi. pergit ad la
cum magnum et ingreditur usque ad ubera et ibidem par
turit super aquam et hoc propter draconem facit presidia

In 1886 Charles F. Holder devoted only one of twenty-five chapters of his superb book, *The Ivory King*, to the African elephant. And then in 1979 Walt Disney made this seemingly trite observation: 'Not all elephants are born in Africa; there are some in Asia, too.' In less than a hundred years, Western civilization had forgotten Asia and shifted the spotlight to black Africa.

CHAPTER 3
THE MEMORY OF THE WEST

The 2nd-century *Physiologus* (left) was widely disseminated in the West from the 12th to the 15th century. In it is the story of an elephant who cannot breed without the fruit of the mandrake, which his mate, a latter-day Eve, has tasted and offers to him. Immediately impregnated, she looks for a large lake where she gives birth. Right: an elephant hard at work in Ceylon around 1900.

LA CHARRUE.   Le labourage à Ceylan.

VÉRITABLE EXTRAIT DE VIANDE LIEBIG.

Our collective memory of elephants is rooted in more than just the Indian individuals that were studied and immortalized by Aristotle, founder of all science and tutor of Alexander the Great. We must not forget the indelible imprint made by the elephants Hannibal marshalled from northern Africa – which at one point caused the fate of Rome to hang in the balance – or the ones the Carthaginian navigator Hanno had already sighted along the Atlantic coast of Morocco, or the ones that, according to Greco-Roman commentators, were blessed by the gods and died at a ripe old age in the forests of the Atlas Mountains.

Historical zoology

Ancient writers probably did not distinguish between the two elephant genera, but the observations they did make were astonishingly detailed. To begin with, there was universal acceptance of the view that African elephants were smaller, weaker and more easily intimidated on the battlefield than Asian ones. In terms of size, the so-called 'African elephant' ranked between the Asian elephant and the large Mycenaean horse. Pyrrhus' Indian elephants were long referred to as 'Lucanian oxen'. At the time there may have existed subspecies, now extinct, among the living species as we know them (which, theoretically at least, do not interbreed).

The hypothesis that a dwarf elephant (christened *Pumilio*) may have survived to modern times has been discredited for decades, but a round-eared animal

Pictures of elephants from the Greco-Roman world (left) are far more accurate than those from the medieval West; the West lost contact with the animal for nearly a thousand years. The Byzantines were not only closer to their classical sources but had occasion to see specimens from India or Ethiopia. The animal pictured here has an atrophied tail, flat back, suction-cup trunk and the tusks of a boar; but the feet, ears and overall bulk are reasonably correct and considerably closer to reality than the aberrations in the *Physiologus*.

2–2.4 metres tall is believed to have evolved from diminutive forest elephants native to Ethiopia or Mauretania. Physically they might have been comparable to – but ought not to be confused with – the ones that were still being sighted in desert regions of Ethiopia as recently as the late 19th century.

Separated from their kin by the rapid desertification of Egypt and the Sahara, their backs to the Atlantic and the Mediterranean, the elephants of northwestern Africa may have evolved smaller forms, possibly due to excessive inbreeding through decreasing numbers. Perhaps that is why they were said to be no match for big Indian elephant bulls that stood 3 metres tall and were highly trained for warfare. By the same token, a match between a forest elephant and a rhinoceros must have made for a less predictable, and therefore more riveting, spectacle in the Roman Circus than the guaranteed victory of a gigantic bush elephant!

The wellsprings of knowledge: the Middle and Near East

We know from Neolithic cave paintings that elephants roamed predynastic Egypt. They probably disappeared

The animals Orpheus is holding spellbound include birds, both exotic and commonplace (owl, peacock), but most are mammals that the mosaicists reduced to roughly the same size: a boar with protruding teeth, a lean mountain bear, a powerfully built spotted cat with a lion's head and muscular neck (a Maghreb leopard?), a horselike animal akin to a wild ass, or dziggetai and a stag with a big set of antlers. The flat-backed elephant with small, round ears and very short tusks comes as something of a surprise. The decor suggests deciduous woodland such as that which must have existed in North Africa in Roman times.

from that area by the end of the 4th millennium BC, together with the rhinoceros and the giraffe. Ivory was virtually the only part of elephants known to the early dynasties, although Sesostris I and Queen Hatshepsut may have sent expeditions to Nubia and Punt (modern Eritrea and Somalia), respectively, and their successors are known to have hunted elephants in Syria. Thutmose III (1504–1450 BC) reportedly slew 120 elephants – for their tusks, of course! – and one of his officers, Amenemhab, saved the pharaoh's life by cutting off a threatening trunk. In addition, a painting in the tomb of his vizier Rekhmire shows an Indian elephant with very long tusks, but tiny in stature next to the disproportionately large men and animals, especially the horses.

Evidence that elephants existed in Mesopotamia dates back to the early 2nd millennium BC (bones found at Babylon, tusks at Megiddo); but there were no more than a few, probably tame individuals that may have been imported from Persia or the Indus valley civilizations.

The Assyrian king Tiglath-Pileser I is known to have hunted elephants on the outer reaches of the Hittite world in the 12th century BC. In 879 BC, Assurnasirpal II collected entire herds and kept them in a 'zoo'. A stele from the early 9th century BC records one of his most impressive hauls: 30 elephants, 450 mighty tigers and 200 ostriches. In the late 8th century BC elephant hides were part of the tribute paid to King Sennacherib. The 'Syrian' elephant seems to have disappeared around this time. Probably in retreat or debilitated by climatic changes, it may have been wiped out by hunting and the growing demand for ivory.

War elephants: Alexander the Great v. King Porus of India

War elephants left a lasting imprint on the memory of the West. A brief overview of their history is imperative – a task simplified by the fact that a great many

The Persian king Cambyses defeated the Egyptians at the Battle of Pelusium (525 BC), captured Pharaoh Psamtik III and ordered his execution. In this re-creation set at the foot of the Sphinx and the Pyramids, elephants from the East are shown clustered in a single, dark mass to the right. All of the details of local colour sprang as much from the painter's vivid imagination as from the 'historical literacy' that certain 19th-century artists cultivated after Napoleon's epic expedition to the Near East.

historians dealt with the subject. It all began with Alexander the Great, whose first encounter with war elephants had occurred in 331 BC: Darius, king of the Persians, fielded fifteen of them at Gaugamela. In 326 BC the Indian king Porus massed 200 elephants, 50,000 infantrymen, 4000 cavalrymen and 300 war chariots on the banks of the Hydaspes. Alexander's horsemen knocked out Porus' cavalry; the Persian chariots were overpowered and routed by 1000 mounted archers. The Macedonian phalanx then advanced to meet the terrifying elephants head on. They encircled individual animals, wounded them with volleys of arrows,

The obelisk of Shalmaneser III (859–824 BC) celebrates his victories (detail).

javelins and long pikes, slashed their trunks with scimitars, killed their mahouts and finally drove the exhausted beasts back on their own troops.

After a final elephant charge led by Porus himself was repulsed, the surviving elephants retreated, pitching like boats at sea. Eighty of them were captured. Porus' elephant reportedly died defending its wounded master; the battle also claimed Alexander's legendary horse, Bucephalus. The heavy losses the Macedonians suffered during their clash with the elephant corps may well have prompted their famous refusal to follow Alexander into the heart of India, where fresh contingents of troops and elephants reportedly awaited them. The two hundred elephants Alexander eventually amassed were never deployed, and the battle they were poised to fight was never joined.

The Battle of the Hydaspes had other repercussions that may not have changed the course of human history, but it proved of great significance in the history of the elephant. Impressed by the strength and power of this new weapon, Alexander's generals and successors incorporated the colossal beasts into their armies and fielded them during the fratricidal wars that broke out after the conqueror's death in 323 BC.

With their backs to India, Macedonian general

This Etruscan plate undoubtedly dates from the time when Pyrrhus was sending Asian elephants into battle, probably equipped with towers. But the Asian cow depicted here (small ears, rounded back) has been endowed with the tusks and a very long tail peculiar to African elephants.

Seleucus and his allies tried to prevent elephants from falling into the hands of their foes; Ptolemy was compelled to turn to Africa for his supply and threw smaller Ethiopian elephants into battle against Indian ones. If the allies carried the day at the Battle of Ipsus (301 BC), it was because of the record five hundred elephants that Seleucus had obtained from the powerful Indian king Chandragupta to bolster the forces marshalled against Antigonus I, formerly a general of Alexander the Great.

Pyrrhus, master tactician, pits elephants against legionaries

Rome's first encounter with war elephants occurred in 280 BC, the year the city of Tarentum appealed to Pyrrhus, king of Epirus and veteran of Ipsus, to help it counter the Roman threat. The eminent tactician turned up with 25,000 troops and 20 elephants. The initial battle was joined at Heraclea, site of the first encounter between the renowned Macedonian phalanx (Alexander had died only forty-three years earlier) and

The Persians familiarized themselves with war elephants and then deployed them when their expansion took them to the doorstep of India. Cornered, Darius fielded fifteen of them against Alexander at Gaugamela. Although they were not properly trained to act in conjunction with cavalry and did not have the anticipated effect, at least they helped cover the great monarch's retreat. Scenes of Alexander's next great battle, *Alexander and Porus*, by Charles Lebrun (opposite), and Watteau's *The Defeat of Porus* (above).

what would soon become the invincible Roman legion. As a result, both sides suffered tremendous losses during repeated clashes of legendary ferocity. Pyrrhus' inspired strategy was to throw his elephants into battle last. The animals, possibly bearing towers with soldiers and archers in them, wreaked havoc among the Roman horses, cavalrymen and foot soldiers. Pyrrhus then sent in his reserve of Thessalian cavalry to complete the rout.

Pyrrhus advanced to within a few miles of Rome, but Italy would not rally to his cause. During the second battle, the Romans fared even worse, losing two legions out of four. After a number of skirmishes with

In 255 BC the Roman consul Regulus landed in Africa and laid down peace terms Carthage could not accept. When the decisive battle was joined, the leader of the Punic forces ordered his cavalry to encircle the Roman lines. The legionaries were trampled by a hundred elephants and finished off by Carthaginian infantry. Regulus was brought in chains to the city he thought he already controlled. At Zama (202 BC) Carthage's elephants turned against their own troops, enabling Rome's allies to swing the battle in Scipio's favour. The battle would inspire artists centuries later.

Carthaginian forces in Sicily, Pyrrhus again engaged the Romans, at Beneventum. Although he lost the battle, his elephants staged a ferocious counterattack that covered his retreat. A final word about this brilliant strategist: his own elephants proved to be his undoing. During the assault on Argos, his elephants, with their towers, could not negotiate the streets. One of them became enraged when its mahout was wounded; it blocked the main thoroughfare, obstructing traffic. Pyrrhus, already wounded, was finished off by a soldier.

The Punic Wars

The Carthaginians had no elephants in 310 BC, the year Agathocles, the tyrant of Syracuse, invaded their African homeland. They decided that a more effective weapon was needed and started building up an elephant corps, possibly taking their cue from the kingdoms of the Hellenistic world. At any rate, by 263 BC, just before the first documented clash in Sicily, Hanno had fifty to sixty trained elephants under his command. After a disastrous defeat in Africa (255 BC), Roman forces in Sicily were extremely reluctant to confront contingents of these colossal beasts.

Then, in 250 BC, when Roman consul Metellus went on the offensive at Panormus (Palermo), he deployed specially armed advance detachments to pick off the mahouts, then to harass, distract, outflank and attack their mounts with javelins, arrows and pikes. The strategy worked. The wounded elephants turned back on their own troops. A number of them were captured with their riders; 104 in all were rounded up and transported back to Rome. After they were paraded in the consul's triumphal procession, most were slaughtered in the Circus, either for revenge or to prove that they were not invulnerable.

Hannibal crosses the Alps

Resolved to pursue the war on Italian soil more than three

Nature threw up major obstacles in the face of Hannibal's epic expedition. Reasonably good swimmers in calm water, elephants have trouble negotiating rivers with as strong a current as the Rhône. Pairs of rafts had to be lashed together to form a pontoon-like structure roughly 30 x 60 metres. Secured to the riverbank, this projecting platform was camouflaged with soil so that its wobbly surface would not frighten the elephants. The animals followed the lead females across the stationary rafts and on to towable rafts designed to ferry them to the other side of the river.

decades later, Hannibal set out from Spain in 219 BC with thirty-seven obviously well-trained elephants. He knew that enough time had elapsed since legionaries last engaged elephants in battle so that the younger generation of Roman soldiers would never have seen them before. The sheer distance of the Carthaginians' trek and the countless obstacles that lay before them turned their expedition into an exploit of truly epic proportions. After crossing the Pyrenees without mishap through the Perthus Pass, they came up against their first real barrier, the Rhône. Some of the elephants were ferried across on rafts; others swam to

Then, a dreadful moment of panic. Some of the elephants, paralyzed with fear, remained on the rafts and reached the opposite shore without mishap. Others flung themselves into the middle of the river and started to swim across. A few mahouts were drowned, but all thirty-seven elephants made it safely to shore and were poised to brave the Alps.

the opposite bank. Meanwhile, Roman general Scipio had taken an army to Spain to try to cut Hannibal off from his rear, and Sempronius was planning an attack against Carthage itself from his base in Sicily.

For the time being, therefore, the only foe standing in Hannibal's way was nature itself; crossing the Alps proved as much an ordeal as any battle. Aside from the hostility of Allobrogian tribes (a Celtic people of Alpine Gaul), he had to contend with snowfall; marshy, impassable valleys; slippery slopes; and shortages of food and fodder. But his powerful elephants were pressed into service to carry food, move rocks and clear a path for themselves and the horses. The very sight of these peculiar-looking creatures probably deterred Alpine peoples from attacking them.

At long last, 26,000 surviving troops and all thirty-seven elephants emerged into the Po river plain as the year 218 BC drew to a close.

The Battle of the Trebia

While Hannibal's exhausted troops regrouped, Scipio and Sempronius returned posthaste and pooled their forces. The battle was joined on the banks of the Trebia in northwestern Italy under appalling conditions of rain, snow and floods. Weaker in infantry, Hannibal ordered his elephants to charge into the triple-line formation of legionaries, who then found themselves ambushed by a concealed detachment of Carthaginian cavalry and infantry led by his brother Mago. Carthage's victory was complete. Only a handful of Romans managed to escape to Placentia (Piacenza).

After Trebia most of the elephants perished, probably as the result of cold and deprivation. Hannibal, who had lost the sight of one eye to ophthalmia, rode the sole surviving animal. Bigger and

The terrifying elephant charge at the Battle of the Trebia (217 BC) smashed through a triple line of legionaries, almost all of whom were facing the colossal beasts for the very first time. While the mahouts kept their capricious mounts from breaking ranks, archers, probably shooting from wicker towers, weakened the Roman infantry and drove it back to within striking distance of the ambush the Punic cavalry had laid for it.

braver than the others, this elephant, reportedly named Surus ('the Syrian'), is likely to have come from India and is said to have been missing a tusk. This was the inspiration for Juvenal's famous verse *cum Gaetula ducem portaret belua luscum* ('the one-eyed leader was riding on his Gaetulian beast'), among others.

In 202 BC, after their defeat at Zama at the hands of Scipio Africanus, the Carthaginians were forced to surrender all elephants still in their possession and promise not to train any more in future. Consequently,

no elephants were seen on the field of battle during the Third Punic War.

The limitations and disadvantages of war elephants soon becomes apparent

Carthage had won its early victories over troops and horses that by and large had never laid eyes on an elephant. Later on, without the element of surprise, there was no making up for the fact that these unwieldy formations precluded elaborate tactics of any kind. Artificially stimulated, the animals charged straight ahead, trampling everything in their path – troops, stockades, horses. Punic soldiers loosed volleys of arrows, darts, spears and javelins while clutching the elephant's back or while inside a protective wooden or wicker tower (probably invented by Pyrrhus). The mahout himself was in a very exposed position that must have made it difficult for him to keep the animal under control and stop it in mid-charge, much less turn

Consuls who won battles were entitled to lead victorious troops (followed by the vanquished) in triumphal procession through Rome. Curius displayed at just such a triumph four of the eight elephants he had captured from Pyrrhus at Beneventum (275 BC), above.

it around. Thus, elephants actually proved relatively easy to parry and counter. The opposing side could stage a frontal attack with another elephant in the lead, hack at hamstrings with axes, slash through trunks with scimitars and stab flanks with sharpened, broad-tipped javelins. (The *falarica*, a fire-bearing missile dipped in bitumen, pitch and naphtha, which adhered to the skin and caused excruciating pain, was especially effective.) They could bring on such heavy weaponry as catapults and scorpions to hurl chunks of rock capable of crippling or knocking down their targets. In addition, although elephants were exposed to the sights and sounds of war beforehand – they were familiarized with the sound of squealing pigs and the sight of fire – they were incurably apprehensive and unpredictable in battle. Other problems were that they tired easily, had huge appetites and were fussy eaters. They not only required extensive training, but were always difficult to transport, expensive to maintain and hard to replace.

The Roman trade in wild animals for the arena was controlled by prosperous middlemen, some based in Sicily, as this mosaic attests.

If elephants endangered their own troops, they might have to be put out of action. During the Battle of the Metaurus, Carthaginian general Hasdrubal himself is said to have devised a method of killing the animals by driving a chisel down into the neck joint with a mallet.

The impact of war elephants on the Western world was no less extraordinary for being short-lived. The three centuries during which they were used spanned the period from Alexander to Hannibal and Caesar.

Bloody arenas

In India the war elephant's nonmilitary counterpart riveted spectators by fighting with another animal – though it almost never killed. In the West, however, champion elephants were expected to kill whenever possible and, in any event, were slain before the clamouring mob, like the bulls in present-day *corridas*. The triumphs of Curius (275 BC) and Metellus (250 BC) brought dozens of African and Indian elephants to Rome, but we do not know whether they were kept alive for use in war or thrown into the arena along with captive lions, bears and panthers.

The earliest reports of elephants forced to fight in the

Few games were more frequently held or more favourably received by hard-to-please Roman spectators than bouts between animals (tigers, lions, rhinoceroses, bulls) that were not natural enemies and may never have otherwise engaged in individual duels. An uncertain outcome made for a more interesting match. A lone bull might slay a lion deprived of its lionesses; a young elephant separated from its family unit might be overpowered by a tiger, lion or rhinoceros that was compelled to fight. Note the difference in bearing between this elephant and the one in the Orpheus mosaic (page 75).

Circus with bulls date from 99 BC. In 55 BC, during the games given by Pompey to celebrate the opening of his theatre, eighteen elephants were pitted against Gaetulians armed with javelins. In a poignant description Pliny tells how one elephant in particular, suffering from leg wounds and crawling on its knees, managed to keep the pack of human tormentors at bay, and how its wretched brethren in the enclosure seemed to cry out for mercy by trumpeting and waving their trunks as if betrayed. Their African mahouts, the story goes, had been given assurances that no harm would come to them.

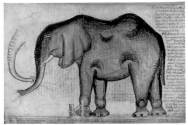

Cicero (106–43 BC), who was an eyewitness, reports that the Roman mob derived no pleasure from this spectacle; in the following century, Seneca commented that the creature had 'a fellowship with the human race'. Under Claudius and Nero, an individual duel with an elephant marked the highpoint – and not infrequently the end – of a gladiator's career. The emperor Commodus is said to have killed three of them himself in the arena.

The elephant as a symbol of piety and devotion

The piety ascribed to elephants carried over into the Christian world and gave rise to various legends. Some reportedly crossed themselves with their trunks or humbly bowed their heads when passing in front of a church. Their devoutness was emphasized even more during the Middle Ages. Elephants, it was believed, sprayed themselves with water in the moonlight. Paragons of propriety, they were said to mate discreetly under a veil of water. They came to be associated with the story of Adam and Eve as well as with Marian

The only thing the medieval West remembered about elephants was that they had a trunk and tusks. The inaccurate illustrations (top and bottom) contrast with Matthew Paris' drawing from life of the animal Louis IX of France gave to his brother-in-law, Henry III of England (centre). It is not an Indian elephant, as one might expect, but a young African specimen.

symbolism. Like the Virgin Mary, they trampled to
death the fiendish snake so that their young might be
protected and Good might triumph over Evil.

The elephant becomes a rarity and a curiosity

By the Middle Ages elephants were no longer being
used in war, for public spectacle or as status symbols;
as a result, practically all meaningful contact between
them and Western people ceased. Less and less was
known about the physical appearance of the animal
that classical and Christian traditions, oral and written
alike, had dealt with so thoroughly. They were pictured
with flat, drooping ears, fanglike canines and broad,
piglike snouts, making them increasingly unrecog-
nizable. Elephants themselves became exceedingly rare.
We know through historians' accounts that one doubly
imperial elephant, a gift from Harun al-Rashid to
Charlemagne, was unloaded at Porto Pisano and
transported to Aix-la-Chapelle to general
amazement. This elephant, Abul Abbas, lived
nearly ten years in Austrasia, east of Gaul.

In 1254 Louis IX of France (St Louis) presented his royal brother-in-law, Henry III of England, with a magnificent specimen he had brought back from the Middle East. It made such an impression on Matthew Paris that the historiographer sketched it from life, once in the *Chronica majora* and again in the *Lives of the Abbots of St Albans*. As a footnote – when Manuel of Portugal presented the pope with an elephant from India, the animal spotted a vessel filled with water and sprayed the assembled dignitaries. Louis XIV was also the recipient of an elephant, which he ordered to be painstakingly dissected after its death.

The Dutch East India Company donated a pair of elephants, Hans and Parkie, to the people of Holland in 1803. The playful, affectionate couple was kept in a kind of menagerie until French troops abducted them and transported them to Paris. During the elephants' journey to the capital, people turned out in droves to see them as they passed through.

The Elephant of the Bastille is the place Gavroche called home in *Les Misérables*: 'At night, the broad brow of the colossus, its trunk, tusks, tower, huge hindquarters and four pillar-like legs stood out, astonishing and awesome, against the starry sky.' Napoleon ordered the elephant to be built in 1813 as the centrepiece of what was to have been a fountain.

Gradually, as the 19th century wore on, both zoo and circus elephants became less of a rarity in the West. Now people could see for themselves that there was something to the age-old descriptions of elephants after all, that their behaviour and that of humans had a great deal in common.

Elephants on stage: prelude to the modern circus

This affinity with people was particularly obvious on stage, where elephants struck ludicrous or clownish poses and mimicked audiences that reacted, not with primitive savagery and bloodlust, but with the benign gentleness of laughter. According to Pliny and Aelian, elephants in classical times were trained to step to music, dance in single file (much like a line of chorus girls or majorettes) and eat with consummate delicacy, using their trunks as hands; they could also walk on tightropes, fling pebbles, hurl weapons and mimic men crowding around a woman in labour. These tricks were precursors of present-day circus acts.

For many years, the Berlin Zoo set the standard for the Western world. Asian elephants were favourites of children and nannies. The introduction of more temperamental African elephants precluded any further physical contact between elephant trunks and human beings.

In the 19th century in France, the Franconi Circus featured Baba, an elephant that sat down at a table, placed a napkin around its neck and uncorked a bottle. P. T. Barnum's elephant drank, pretended to be tipsy and played tricks on a man whose job it was to act the fool in front of an elephant that pretended to be human. The American showman also 'abducted' the celebrated Jumbo from London; the elephant died at the age of twenty-five in a train accident. By that time, elephants were being trained to balance themselves on a ball and to play soccer or cricket.

Emotions ran high in England when the London Zoo agreed to sell Jumbo to P. T. Barnum for his circus. Americans were largely responsible for turning the elephants that so intrigued zoo-goers into crowd-pleasing animal acts.

The symbolic intent of this picture seems simple enough. The subject is an encounter between a passing boatload of people and an elephant that has ventured into the shallows, trunk raised in greeting. On the one hand, the composition emphasizes the giant's swarthy, erect bulk (extended by its upright trunk) poised between the shimmering water and the cloudy skies, and, on the other, the pale flatness of the floating hideout with its tiny passengers and deadly weapons. The luminous column of water raised by the short shot acts as a dividing line and underscores the vertical link between the animal's uplifted trunk and the boat's super-structures. Perhaps mirroring an age of triumphant colonization, the artist (an Englishman named Barnes, 1858) may not have intended to convey anything other than this compositional contrast. In the context of current events, it is liable to take on an altogether different, and deeper, meaning. Onlookers may project their own readings and preoccupations on to this picture.

The view of the West

The image people had of elephants by the 19th century was devoid of cruelty or unkindness; phrases like 'a memory like an elephant' even carried a hint of admiration. Above all, it should be noted that, among animals, the elephant came to be regarded as the embodiment of positive moral attributes, the majority of which can be traced back to Asia and classical antiquity. Swiss naturalist Conrad Gesner enumerated these alleged virtues in Latin in the 16th century; S. de Priezac (among others) did the same in French with his 17th-century treatise, *Histoire des éléphants.*

The elephant has made its presence felt in everyday life in various ways: one French advertisement for cigarette paper and another for an indestructible mattress.

JE NE FUME QUE LE NIL

PAPIER A CIGARETTES   JOSEPH BARDOU & FILS

In his introduction the author declared the elephant was 'a subject in which moral virtues stand out, polity prevails, integrity is triumphant and torment and punishment the sole reward for vice'. Each successive chapter deals with a particular virtue, each 'substantiated' by Greco-Roman texts or persistent legends: moderation, piety, prudence, pride, tact, affection for its young, respect for its elders, propriety, charity, mercy, presence of mind, intelligence, fidelity, justice.

To this perception of the elephant we must add the deep affection people cannot help but accord this strong, stalwart, kindly and endearingly ungainly giant.

Lately, this ingrained, sentimentalized image has taken on other overtones – no less emotionally charged – which have more to do with the issues of the elephant's environment and how it is changing. Behind the living elephant now looms the spectre of the dead elephant, murdered, along with Mother Nature, by the parricides we refer to as human beings.

RIEN NE LUI RÉSISTE!!......

SAUF LE LIT NORMAL
AU LIT D'OR
56,60, Rue Rombuteau, PARIS III*

Millions of young readers around the world are acquainted with the elephant-king Babar (right).

très content
de ses achats
et satisfait
de son élégance,
Babar va
chez le photographe.

In terms of their reproductive ability, elephants are a dynamic and vigorous lot. A single cow can give birth several times during her long reproductive life; and a high proportion of calves, well protected from predators, can be expected to reach maturity. But predators – especially people – have made huge dents in elephant populations.

CHAPTER 4
FROM SPORT TO SLAUGHTER

Hunting can be a test of manhood. You get to keep the trophy, or you can sell it for a profit, which then leads to more hunting.

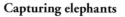

M ost of the elephants captured in Asia were near adult age and could be broken, tamed and domesticated; therefore they had to be captured alive. They might have been driven into a swamp from which they could not escape. Tame elephants would be brought in quickly to calm them down.

Capturing elephants

Century after century, capturing elephants alive inevitably led to the death of some of their family members. Those that were caught sometimes sustained injury and were often unable to erase the image of the free-ranging life they had stored away in their astonishing memory. An estimated 50 per cent of captive elephants ate poorly, unable to adjust to being transported or uprooted from familiar surroundings, succumbed to illness and died of stress or a 'broken heart' within the first weeks of captivity. For every elephant that was hunted and brought back alive for the pleasure of the Roman mob – only to be slain – at least nine are believed to have lost their lives. No wonder the North African stock was depleted by the 3rd century.

Traditional methods for capturing elephants changed little over time. Simple and functional, they were still

being used as recently as the middle of the 20th century by the Moi people of Southeast Asia, for one.

Two non-destructive methods: roundups and harpooning

Large numbers of people were needed to frighten herds and shepherd them towards a huge stockade in a roundup. This process could exact a toll in human life, but not usually in elephants, though occasionally the matriarch of a family unit charged and had to be eliminated. More often she managed to escape, as did the most aggressive bulls, which would be ungovernable and dangerous, in any case. The rest of the herd, distressed by the desertion of their leaders or protectors, converged, panic-stricken, on the corral, and scores of them were channelled into the enclosure. The tall stakes fencing them in (which they could knock down if given enough time) were defended by men who, not without risk, pushed them back with pointed sticks or cold steel. Then, one at a time, prospective trainees were culled from the herd. The oldest and most irascible individuals were released (unharmed), as were rogue elephants, considered impossible to break. The others were subjected to 'calming' fasts and gradually led out with an escort of tame elephants.

This convoy of elephants, captured in Siam (Thailand) before the First World War, is being escorted by large tame bulls and men armed with sharp pikes. Probably weakened by the hunt, especially if they were forced to swim for long periods of time in high water, the captives trudge off to market or the training pen. Here, too, elephants that have already been domesticated are indispensable for calming the captives down (often by their mere presence), teaching by example and, initially at least, breaking them of undesirable habits.

Despite its name and the fact that it probably evolved from the Palaeolithic practice of trapping mammoths in mud, harpooning was (or, at least, was meant to be) another non-destructive technique. It, too, called for crowds of people, large numbers of tame elephants, a great deal of noise-making and lighted torches to help drive the wild elephants out of the hills and on to a low-lying plain. The hunt was deliberately held during the rainy season. As the water gradually rose and the hundreds of elephants tried to escape, they fell foul of each other instead, not daring to challenge the awesome barrier of tame elephants that had been mustered from many surrounding villages. The water continued to rise, and before long – with only the tallest trees poking through the surface – the wild elephants had no alternative but to swim. Harpooners in canoes then hurled iron hooks into the thickest part of the elephants' ears, and each captive was securely tethered to a sturdy tree. The elephants wore themselves out swimming in circles; this had a calming effect. After some time a rattan cradle was slipped under their bellies to support them and keep them from drowning.

A far more athletic and dangerous technique

Lassoing could be used only to capture elephants singly, but it made for a particularly exciting hunt. It, too, required extraordinary teamwork with tame elephants that had been thoroughly trained and, in this case, divided into three groups. The first, the 'beaters', prevented the wild animals, once driven into the open, from bolting into the woods. The more specialized 'catchers' nudged the rear end of a selected individual with their broad foreheads in such a way that the mahout was able to slip a noose around its hind foot. The captive was tethered to a sturdy tree but could swing around to charge. Time for the 'fighters': their job was to suppress such charges and allay the fears of their wild brothers. Now and again, the battle spread, for the wild herd might try to come to a captive's assistance. To guard against this possibility, all the

Lassoing elephants in 18th-century Burma. In the foreground two heavily tusked 'catchers' nudge a recalcitrant wild elephant from behind until one of the mahouts is able to slip a noose around one of its hind feet. The elephant in the middle distance, realizing that it has been lassoed, has started to bolt, but, restrained by a large tame elephant, is about to fall. An old female, probably the matriarch, has already

villages in the vicinity were required to marshal their full complement of 'fighters' ahead of time so that the tame animals would outnumber the wild ones and thus be able to overpower them. Extremely strong and skilful, these massive bull elephants could stun smaller aggressive bulls with their trunks, thwart charges with their bodies or their tusks (the tips of which are usually blunted or sawn off) and do battle with the ringleaders. Thanks to them, there was a minimum of bloodshed.

Femmes fatales

Another method for taking individual elephants, although singularly benign, roused the righteous

swung around and raised her trunk in preparation for a possible attack. The elephant in the background, its foot already lassoed, has swung around to fight. A 'fighter' intervenes and thwarts the attack with its tusks, while the mahout uses a pike to fend off blows from its fearsome trunk.

indignation of upstanding Anglo-Saxons in the late
1800s because it tricked this noble beast with foul play
and deception of the lowest sort: the use of female
temptresses to lure bull elephants into captivity. These
domesticated cows did not simply wait for an
unsuspecting victim to succumb to their wiles, but they
actively solicited him at the urging of a mahout, hidden
under a saddlecloth to disguise his scent.

Their mission was to entice, lead on and above all
tire out a victim. They would take turns for several days
running, always keeping him awake; men stood by and
made noise the moment the bull showed signs of falling
asleep.

Overcome, the inveigled 'macho' eventually dropped
from exhaustion and awoke to find a heavy shackle
around his hind leg. The trainers immediately went to
work, while the femmes fatales trudged off in pursuit of
another hapless dupe.

To pacify mortified Anglo-Saxon readers, treatises on
the subject fortunately mentioned that less scandalous
outcomes were possible. After training, a big bull
elephant might find himself back among these false-
hearted Jezebels and, far from showing his
displeasure, offer himself to those cows
willing to accept his proposal. The
result: a fairy-tale ending, with
bouncing baby elephants.

The historian Arrian (AD
95–175) reports another
Indian practice.
Cows in oestrus
were grouped
at one end of
a narrow
bridge to lure
bulls, which
were then
trapped,
unable to
turn back.

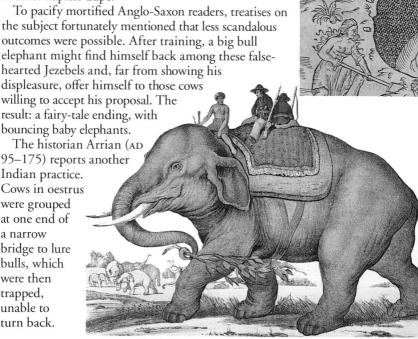

The pitfall method calls for both tame elephants and a large contingent of humans. The narrow circular pit into which this full-grown (and therefore dangerous) bull has fallen is free from sharp, poison-tipped stakes or other instruments of death. The process of extricating him would prove too much for straps, girths or ropes, and would snap the big log that has been rigged up as a primitive pulley. The purpose of this apparatus is merely to steady the victim and prevent it from swinging around, for as the men come into view it may try to knock them senseless with its trunk or gore them with its tusks. As earth is gradually shovelled in to raise the level of the pit floor, the animal finds itself face to face with its captive brothers.

Other methods were deadlier

In Mysore, southern India, the method was to capture an elephant alive in a deep hole – a pitfall. Very often the victim would break its leg or end up crushed by another elephant attempting to help it. Moreover, since removing a captive from the hole was a difficult, time-consuming task, it was forced to endure periods of boredom and fasting. The African version of the pitfall was virtually the same, except that it was designed to kill. The bottom of the pit would often be strewn with pieces of pointed bamboo or poisoned stakes.

Hunting to kill

Eastern civilizations seldom sought to kill elephants. They realized that a live elephant was far more

Full-grown but not too advanced in years, this magnificent 'fighter' bull (left) has stout tusks, a sound, robust body and a decisive gait. He has been trained to cooperate unconditionally with its mahout and two assistants.

appealing than a dead one, especially since whatever products it might provide could be salvaged anyway after a more or less normal lifespan. (A case in point: the highest-quality ivory comes from tusks allowed to grow to maximum size.) But these civilizations did their fair share of killing, just the same – and not just detachments of war elephants left unclaimed on the field of battle. Rogues, if not entire herds, had to be eliminated if aggressiveness or resulting damage turned them into nuisances. To this end Asia devised destructive methods comparable to those used in Africa.

Lethal traps were roughly the same in Asia and Africa. An elephant walking under a tree might trigger the release of a very heavy wooden log studded with sharp barbs, breaking its neck. A huge, poison-tipped arrow might be shot from a gigantic crossbow, or a herd might be driven on to planks studded with poisoned barbs that dug into their feet. The foot fetter – a thin, hollow device studded with sharp bamboo tips pointing in and down – was fastened to a big, heavy block of wood. Once caught, the elephant could not remove its foot and would tire from dragging the

These diminutive men have managed to kill an unusually large elephant. Attacking the animals from behind with axes would be inconceivable unless the animals were unable to swing around.

Sic foſsis for

heavy block. It would then be finished off with assegais.

Pygmies coated themselves with elephant dung to disguise their scent and disembowelled their quarry alive with spears, a dangerous sport they regarded as a test of manliness and a rite of passage to adulthood. In the vicinity of Ethiopia, hunters reportedly severed the animal's hind leg tendons so that it could neither bolt nor charge, and they shot poisoned arrows at the base of its ear, the inside of its limbs and even into its gut. The poison, related to digitalis, induced acute heart failure fairly quickly.

The 'pupu' rifle was typically used in black Africa. A substantial amount of gunpowder was loaded into the muzzle; when discharged, the firearm would scatter point-blank an unlikely assortment of nails, bolts, bits of lead and bullets. It seldom killed and often injured as many people as elephants; if unharmed, the elephant would turn suspicious or vicious, or, if injured, wander far away to die a useless death. Some of these methods were extremely destructive and resulted in totally pointless carnage.

We do not know how close this engraving comes to the truth, but if we credit the Latin inscription, the only thing missing is the 'shrillness' of the 'tremendous' cries which preside over the slaughter of these 'bands of elephants' that are being enticed into water-filled pitfalls and finished off with pikes. The scattered tusks in the foreground suggest that the lure of ivory was the main reason for this massacre. Swift, well-trained horses are known to have been used to put elephants to flight, especially if their riders shouted. But the final phase – the kill – cannot have been easy using this method.

From noble sport to undisguised slaughter

A hunter puts his life in jeopardy when he confronts a dangerous animal, be it wild cat, snake or elephant.

Eridore Elephantes   *Agmine cōnemunt, capiuntur cuſpidis ictu.*

An elephant roundup in northwestern Ceylon (Sri Lanka)

This account of a roundup was written in 1924 by the French consul to Colombo and published with original photographs in *L'Illustration,* a French periodical. The elephants there had not been hunted in more than four years and had wreaked considerable havoc. Instead of killing them, however, the authorities decided that a certain number of them should be captured and put to work. The plan was for hundreds of 'beaters' to locate and encircle wild herds over a period of three to four months, then, with a minimum of noise, slowly shepherd them into a funnel-shaped structure that forced the animals through the narrow gate of a *kraal,* a very sturdy enclosure of posts reinforced with a framework of horizontal and slanting struts (left). Here the final phase of the roundup would take place while people from nearby towns and villages looked on. The human was never completely impassable; occasionally a strapping bull managed to break through. Uncooperative rogue elephants that never stopped charging would have to be weeded out.

The roundup unfolds

The 'beaters' worked in shifts, keeping watch or slowly but surely driving the herds forward. With thousands of people crowding in from both sides, the bulk of the herd was manoeuvred to the entrance to the funnel, where they were crammed together, jostled and flustered by trumpeting and charging rogue elephants. Once they cleared the gate, the elephants were able to relax in a small pond inside the *kraal* (left). This process claimed only one life: an elephant calf drowned in the joyous commotion at the pond. Next, tame elephants would be introduced into the mix (below).

Enter the tame elephants

As onlookers watched, a contingent of twenty-odd well-trained elephants led by a huge bull proceeded to subdue the forty wild elephants. The captives dared not challenge them as a herd and retreated to the rear of the *kraal*. As they fell back, each individual was encircled and a noose slipped around one of its feet. A large bull pulled it along, two others acted as an escort and some men tethered it to a tree.

If the hunter lost his life, his sacrifice was seen as ennobling in many cultures. He did so of his own free will so that the community might be delivered from mortal danger. A Pygmy who ventured all alone between an elephant's legs to disembowel it with a spear displayed extraordinary courage. Sometimes it cost him his life; by then the herd, perhaps the prospective victim itself, may have already claimed several of the 'beaters' who had encircled and isolated his quarry. In the 19th and early 20th centuries elephants given a fighting chance killed their share of white hunters in Africa – even when they were extremely well armed and attended – as well as a number of noblemen in India and Indochina.

Today, while elephant hunting is highly restricted, it is still permitted in a few countries with healthy herds. Some people – the kind that show off trophies to gratify their egos and crave undeserved admiration for bravery they do not possess – are intent on killing mighty beasts without running the slightest risk. Hunting with an arsenal of firearms and explosive bullets is tantamount to premeditated murder. And what about the safaris of hired killers, or people with nothing better to do, who hunt with machine guns from helicopters? Elephant carcasses rot in the sun, and orphaned calves die within a few days. If it is not safe to land, the coveted tusks might even go unclaimed.

Ivory, the elephant's curse

To begin with, obtaining ivory need not entail the brutal

The widespread use of guns and explosive bullets ushered in the age of the great white hunter. Here we see one posing complacently on top of a fallen elephant and surrounded by the five men he has armed.

death and wholesale slaughter of elephants. There are other ways to acquire it than to massacre the wild herds.

Fossil ivory from Siberian mammoths is often of remarkable size and quality. The tusks of elephants allowed to die a natural death – their lifespans often extended by protective measures – are particularly large and, upon the animal's demise, can be harvested by guards or owners who do no violence and commit no crime. This practice, which has always existed for the large, tame (sometimes sacred) bull elephants of Asia, has become commonplace in closely supervised game reserves in Africa.

In addition, many Asian elephants often have the tips of their tusks sawn off, a practice that not only prevents accidents or skirmishes when they come into musth, but helps make the main part of the tusk bigger and stronger. Whole tusks might even be removed from living animals by means of a fairly routine surgical procedure. Currently, this is one way of protecting a faithful companion and able assistant from poachers;

Some trophies were particularly inventive. It all depended on the taste and wallet of the purchaser or the hunter in his hire. Think of the painstaking work, imagination and money that went into this whole stuffed elephant head. In this case its ears were not turned into coffee tables, its feet into umbrella stands or its tusks into billiard balls.

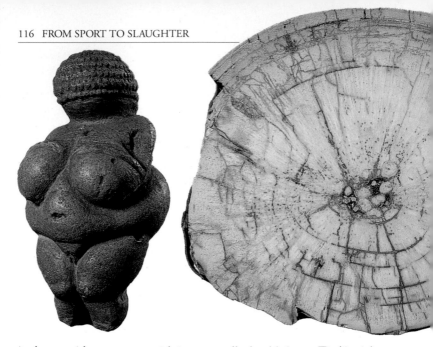

it also provides an owner with ivory to sell, should the need arise, while the animal is still alive. Nor is it unusual to find and collect tusks that have broken off clean and been left behind by their bearers after a skirmish with another elephant or a tug-of-war with a tree's leathery bark or huge, stubborn roots.

Times have changed. Until the 19th century ivory was regarded as a by-product of an animal that was killed primarily for its meat, because it proved a 'nuisance', or in time of war, because it was an adversary – but not for the sole purpose of obtaining tusks. Historical fluctuations in elephant stocks were due to many factors, not to ivory alone, and elephants were not endangered by the trade in ivory until modern times.

For example, the fact that mammoths bore tusks obviously did not bring about their extinction. Humans simply availed themselves of the ivory from dead or slain individuals and turned them into crude statues, handles or daggers and sundry weapons and implements, just as they did with reindeer antlers and

Prehistoric humans used huge mammoth bones to brace the walls of their dwellings and mammoth ivory (cross-section of mammoth tusk, above) to carve figures. Witness the Venus of Willendorf (above left). Mesopotamian civilizations also favoured ivory for radiant female heads whose enigmatic, timeless smiles (above right) rival that of the Mona Lisa.

It is estimated that between 1825 and 1914, until the completion of the Trans-Siberian Railway, at least 2000 metric tons of mammoth ivory passed through Yakutsk alone. By some accounts, the figure for the period 1860–1900 was as high as 50 metric tons a year. How many hundreds, perhaps thousands of tons are stockpiled in the permanently frozen ground of Siberia and other regions? Determined to safeguard its patrimony, the Soviet Union has gradually banned the official export of mammoth tusks, especially since the Second World War, which caused the price of ivory to jump. Illicit trade in mammoth ivory may not only make it possible to dispose of otherwise unmarketable reserves of elephant ivory, but also spur a resumption of the slaughter by way of the Ivory Coast and Taiwan, neither of which was among the 103 signatories to the Convention on International Trade in Endangered Species that became effective in January 1990.

unusually hard bones. To a certain extent, this was also true of much later Chinese ivory work, wonderful pieces often carved out of fossil tusks from the outer reaches of the north Asian tundra.

The use of fossil ivory may have helped spread the practice of using ivory from living elephants; since the supply of fossil ivory could not keep pace with growing demand, Asian wild ivory had to be supplemented with ivory from Africa. Thus was set in motion the disastrous sequence of events culminating in excessive Chinese and Japanese demand. Although this prompted a ban on all trade in ivory (effective 18 January 1990), no provision was made for fossil ivory. The Soviet Union, for example, has extensive reserves of this natural resource, and large quantities may lie undiscovered in Canada or Alaska.

Africa the innocent

Considering the ways in which one Old World civilization after another has exploited ivory over the centuries, we can safely say that no region has made less use of it than Africa. According to Polybius (as reported by Pliny), natives in the vicinity of Ethiopia turned 'elephant teeth' into fences and door jambs (ivory is extremely durable, even termite-proof), but these 'teeth' were clearly by-products; so were the pieces of jewelry or hunting, battle and signalling horns these people in the land of big elephants were content to fashion from small tusks. Local tribespeople were undoubtedly skilled at working this white gold, but never attempted to use more than nature made available to them.

Then in the late 15th century the Portuguese fostered the growth of ivory crafts in the kingdom of Benin, and it was not long before the sovereign chief (*oba*), who received one elephant tusk for every animal taken, started dealing in raw, unwrought ivory. In any case, the people who dealt in dead elephants made minimal use of their ivory themselves. They may have had a hand in slaughtering the animals, but it was at the instigation of non-African civilizations.

The Portuguese were the first to reach black Africa from the West. In the course of their sailing around the continent, they also became the first to explore East Africa from Zanzibar to Oman, where Arab sultans had already established an organized trade in ivory and slaves. Thus, to the gold were added profits from both 'black' and 'white' trade, not only with the American colonies and European craftsmen, but with the Muslim world and the Far East.

Asia, on the other hand, has always been a heavy ivory user

It would be impossible to retrace here the five-thousand-year-long history of ivory carving in Asia, which began with the civilizations of the Indus valley and ancient China. The substance was used in everything from thrones and chieftains' chairs to dagger and sword handles.

China and Japan were also responsible for the most recent ivory rush (after 1960). Demand for musical instruments, belt buckles, piano keys and, most of all, signature seals (two million of them for Japan alone in 1988) precipitated the annual slaughter of 100 thousand elephants. By then, large elephants had been all but wiped out.

From ancient artefacts to piano keys

For a very long time, Westerners made use of ivory they themselves did not produce. Furniture with ivory veneers was found at Erech (Mesopotamia) during the 2nd and 1st millennia BC; the Canaanites and Assyrians turned

I vory from the western woodlands was worked and carved by the gifted sculptors of Benin, and ivory from the eastern savannas was harvested for purchase and export. This led to a rapid upswing in demand, quickly followed by supply. Local potentates built up personal reserves of ivory. The simplest way of gaining access to them was to present tribal chiefs with offerings of coveted goods from Europe; they would return the favour with gifts of their own. The higher a chief's rank, the more gifts he received and the more warriors and subjects he could summon for the exchange, which took place amongst the dazzling pageantry of ceremonial parasols and the flags of England, Holland and other 'protectors'.

out tablets with relief carvings of religious scenes
as well as small carved caskets. Although
elephants still roamed the region, ivory
was probably also brought in from
India and Africa by way of Egypt
and the Red Sea at that time.
Indeed, quite a few texts and
artefacts allude to the land of
Punt (Somalia) as far back as
the 2nd millennium BC.
Homeric descriptions of
thrones or beds partially made
of ivory; Tutankhamun's chair;
King Solomon's gold and ivory
throne; and the renowned
chryselephantine statues of Zeus at
Olympia and Athena Parthenon in
Athens – both by the incomparable
Phidias – all bear witness to the use
of ivory. Religious subjects inspired most
of what Rome, Byzantium and the
Christian West produced, but a number
of natural subjects (plants, animals)
turned up here and there: on book covers,
ivory hunting horns, caskets, boxes,
bishops' croziers, combs, chessmen.
In addition, inlaid pulpits and mosque
doors were produced in the Muslim world.

During the 18th century the influence
of Chinese and Indian work enhanced the
appeal of ivory in the West. In addition to
countless chinoiseries, artisans turned out
objects for everyday use (snuffboxes, dagger
handles, rifle butts, large-eyed needles, toilet
and sewing articles, dominoes, sweet boxes and
fans), not to mention innumerable Christ
figures and statues. Massive quantities of ivory
were diverted early on for piano keys, although
the substance served no immediate artistic
purpose and could just as easily have been

The size of tusks
precluded the
carving of large ivory
pieces – hence its use
in inlay work and small
plaques. If the subject
called for working on a
large scale, sheets of ivory
were laid side by side over
a wooden core, and then
liquid gold was carefully
poured over them. This
is how the renowned
chryselephantine
statuettes such as the one
on the right were made.

replaced with bone. At the same time, billiards – played with ivory balls – became a fashionable game among aristocrats, the monied, and even crowned heads from Louis XIV to Marie Antoinette; after the French Revolution, it caught on everywhere. Equally popular were the trophies that became tokens of middle-class wealth: bogus tributes to hunting prowess. If the almost total retreat of Asian elephants was ultimately due to pressure on their living space, the slaughter of African elephants was caused almost entirely by demand from non-African countries and organized, large-scale trade networks.

An ivory trade right from the start

The Phoenicians were probably the first to engage in organized ivory trade on a large scale. Their network initially reached towards the Mediterranean, then, through Carthage, expanded into the Mediterranean basin proper. Sub-Saharan and south Saharan ivory was brought in by caravan to Lepcis Magna (Tripolitania) and from there transported to Cairo, Tunis and Morocco throughout the Middle Ages and into the first part of the modern era.

The Portuguese reached the Bight of Benin by sea in the 15th century and ranged through the future Ivory Coast and Slave Coast. Along with shipments of gold, these two commodities were channelled to the Iberian region and the New World; Muslim traders brought them out of the African interior to ports between Zanzibar and Oman, where they were loaded on to boats bound for Arabia, Egypt, Persia, even India and China. As a result of this devastating

With their intrinsic nobility, most ivory pieces were intended for use by the great of this world or for religious purposes: croziers (far left), combs with winged lions, storage caskets (above). The West's most famous ivory pieces date from the Middle Ages (in the reigns of Charlemagne and Otto the Great), but those from India and especially China have always been, and continue to be, a hallmark of Far Eastern art.

traffic towards markets in the West (controlled mainly by Europeans) and the East (controlled mainly by Arabs, who eventually had to compete with the Portuguese in Mozambique), black Africa was drained of both people and elephants. With the two world wars and a drop in ivory demand, the animals enjoyed a reprieve, but demand was spurred anew by a fresh surge in supply, this time provided by guerrillas and marauding soldiers, and emerging nationalist movements strapped for cash. In time these tusks reaped profits for Taiwan and Hong Kong, thanks to superb craftsmanship and a flawlessly organized trade network geared to an affluent clientele. Demand skyrocketed, mainly from their dynamic neighbours, the Japanese.

Fezzes joined forces with pith helmets to induce Africans to obtain ivory for them. Mature tusks 1.5 to 2 metres long – virtually nonexistent today – were still available in the late 19th century.

Poaching today

By the 1960s, ivory suppliers, who were little more than poachers operating outside all international control, had perfected coordinated techniques. They would barricade miles of savanna with tall, thick thornbushes, cut out a few corridors and fill these gaps with snares that indiscriminately claimed large numbers of elephants, giraffes, big cats, zebras and impalas. All of these animals died a lingering death and often became living meals for hyenas, lions and vultures. Poachers made off with any and all marketable body parts: tusks that had been spared

by predators; the tail and hair, to be turned into fly whisks, bracelets, ornaments and thick necklaces worn by graceful Samburu women; feet for umbrella stands; ears for tables and drums; hides for leather, breastplates and now cowboy boots; and even eyelashes, coveted in India because they are believed to guarantee fertility and the desired number of children!

In recent years poachers have come under increasing surveillance and are even themselves being hunted, but with mixed results. Often they have just enough time to seize the tusks, leaving the meat to rot, which attracts predators or compassionate fellow elephants. Other times there have been bloody shootouts with anti-poaching teams, but in many cases, the poachers do their killing unimpeded.

Poaching eliminates bull elephants, pregnant cows and younger animals– all with increasingly lighter tusks – leaving immature herds without guidance,

Two age-old uses for the elephant: ivory and transportation. The earliest tusks from Africa were extremely light: 7 to 9 kilos each.

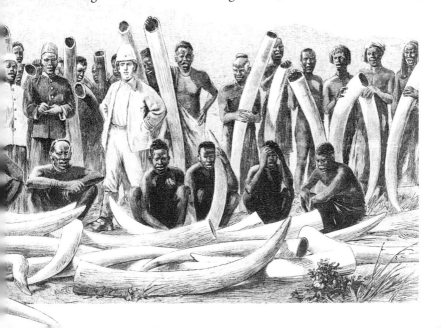

protection, experience or breeding potential, often doomed to die because they do not know the location of foraging grounds or water holes. This carnage, which upsets species demography as well as herd structure, would not have occurred had there been no dealers or buyers. In a few short years, the affluence, greed and fashion consciousness of wealthy countries led to the genocide of the African elephant, that is, the destruction of a species denied survival and reproductive capacity. Declining at an astonishing rate, *Loxodonta* may be on the road to extinction. The only survivors may be residual groups confined to overpopulated preserves where culling would keep destabilized herds within limits that could be sustained by the restricted habitat allotted them. Eventually the largest individuals would be picked off by poachers.

For its part, Asia may be hard-pressed to preserve its fifty thousand surviving elephants, in view of the human population explosion that threatens to overwhelm them.

The sentimentality of the child in all of us is an excellent thing, and we must bear in mind that it is one of the reasons the temporary rescue of the elephant is under way. But we must look into the future. Stopping the slaughter is now considered a matter of urgency – all well and good – but the elephant problem, like that of Africa's endangered environment, will not go away. Let us say that elephant herds are replenished in a few decades. Hundreds of thousands of additional elephants will then have to share a continent with hundreds of millions of additional people: a new elephant problem.

In the short run, of course, highland areas, which for the time being are unsuitable for raising livestock or farming, might prove a heaven on earth for elephants. But it remains to be seen whether their presence would prove a help or a hindrance to humans. Could domestication be the answer? As things stand now, this would be difficult to carry out, of little use and very expensive; it would also require a change in human attitudes.

E lephants can proliferate and prosper when afforded some measure of protection from hunting. But when confined to small pockets of land, they exert too much pressure on plant life.

Surviving elephants must be allowed to roam unrestricted. The hordes of tourists that descend upon, say, Kenya, and which generate more revenue than local agriculture, do so at least in part to watch wild elephants. We must therefore consider alternatives that will ensure the survival of sizable, free-ranging – but monitored – herds.

Regular cropping of large bulls would have little destabilizing effect on herd structure and would provide mountains of meat. But that would necessitate

That is why some countries are currently culling their herds. In a matter of minutes all bulls deemed in excess of sustainable limits can be eliminated.

extremely strict management and – since large bulls have the biggest tusks – once again raise the ivory issue. Countries with available reserves of elephants, and the white gold they bear, are often very poor. It is right that we should help them safeguard their elephants and possibly compensate them for revenue shortfalls resulting from their efforts to preserve a natural heritage that is shared by all humankind. Those who have had a hand in murdering elephants for the sake of fashion should have a hand in protecting them, even if it means absorbing some of the cost of hiring and equipping the necessary gamekeepers.

Elephants are more than just the beloved animals we are rescuing *in extremis* from

"Report from the World Committee for the Defence of Elephants: The following actions have been taken against hunters who have failed to comply with the Committee's directives.... As yet unexecuted: one public thrashing for Mrs Challu, 'champion' of big-game hunting. The Committee reiterates that its mission is limited and unambiguous, namely, the protection of nature –

premeditated murder. They stand for more than hugeness, power, benevolence, justice and the anthropophilia we Westerners have traditionally projected on to the African elephant – the brother of the one we have known for thousands of years, the one whose long childhood, adolescence, adulthood and old age are so much like our own. They reflect our attitude towards nature, that idol with feet of clay, which is now at the mercy of our goodwill. All the fears aroused by the natural world's precarious fate are focused on elephants; at a deeper level, there is the prospect of our world caving in around us. Once they were the pillars of Brahma's universe; today, for a consumer society run amok, elephants are truly the timeless 'roots of heaven'.

starting with elephants – and all animals which textbooks in schools the world over refer to as 'friends of man', and feels that all people, whoever they may be and wherever they may live, can and must cooperate therewith. "

Romain Gary
The Roots of Heaven
1980

DOCUMENTS

The mammoths of Siberia

Alfred Edmund Brehm, 'pope' of descriptive zoology, travelled extensively – from Africa to Siberia – during the second half of the 19th century before writing his study of animals.

The burial grounds of this elephant are found in the lands of the Ostyaks, the Tungus, the Samoyeds and the Burates, along the banks of the Ob river, the Yenisey and the Yena, between 58° N and the Arctic Ocean. When the sandy beaches thaw, one discovers entire mountains of gigantic teeth, mixed with enormous bones. Sometimes, these teeth are firmly implanted in jawbones; some have even been found covered with flesh that is still bloody, hair and skin.

The indigenous peoples called this animal *mammont;* they said it was of an enormous height, 6 to 10 feet; that it had a long, broad head, feet resembling a bear's; that it lived underground; that during its subterranean walks it would at times stick its head above ground and withdraw it immediately, as it found sunlight hurtful; that it ate mud and died if it was ever on sandy soil, because it could not pull its feet out; that it perished as soon as it came into the open air. This was what Ides wrote when, on a diplomatic mission to China in 1692, he heard people speak about these deposits of bones.

The naturalist illustrator Pallas, at the end of the last century, gave us very exact renderings of the fossil remains of the mammoth. But the greatest

Mammoth skeleton exhibited at the National Museum of Natural History in Paris.

discovery in terms of this species was made by Adams, at the mouth of the Lena river. Having learned that a mammoth with its skin and hair had been found, Adams left as soon as possible to salvage the precious remains, joining the Tungus chief responsible for the find. The Tungus had discovered the animal in 1799 but had not touched it, as the ancients told of a similar monster which had been found on the same peninsula, and which had brought a curse on the family of the person who had encountered it; everyone perished. This tale frightened the chief to the point where he became ill. However, the enormous tusks excited his greed, and he resolved to get them. In March 1804 he gave both of them up in exchange for merchandise of little value.

Adams made his voyage two years later; he found the animal in the same spot, yet torn apart. The Yakuts had stripped away the flesh to feed their dogs. Isatis, wolves, wolverines, foxes had fed on it. The skeleton was intact, with the exception of one of its front feet. A dry skin covered its head. An eye and the brain were still there. The feet had their callouses. An ear, covered with silky hair, was equally well preserved. Three-quarters of the skin still existed. This skin was of a dark grey colour; the down covering it was reddish, the bristle black and thicker than the eyelashes of a horse. Adams collected what he could. He skinned the animal, and ten men could barely lift the hide. He had all the hair that was scattered around the ground collected and got almost 38 pounds of it. The entirety was sent to St Petersburg and did not arrive without some deterioration, the skin having lost its hair; nonetheless, thanks to the

Foot of a mammoth found in the Lyakhov Islands, Siberia.

efforts and perseverance of this naturalist, the matter was put beyond all question. The longest hair was from the neck; it measured more than two feet. The rest of the body was covered by an abundant fur, irrefutable proof that the mammoth lived in a cold climate. Its tusks were even more curved than those of elephants living today (some of them traced three-quarters of a circle). Adams saw tusks that measured 23 feet in length.

The discovery of this animal long preoccupied scholars; nobody could explain the sudden disappearance of the beasts of this region. Some, on the basis of vegetal remains, entertained the idea of a sudden change in the earth's axis of rotation; others tended toward the notion of a flood that might have submerged Siberia.

Alfred Edmund Brehm
An Illustrated Study of Animals
'Mammals', vol. 2, 1860

The language of elephants

Nothing is as silent as a majestic procession of elephants passing in front of Mount Kilimanjaro. Yet the air is filled with their call, resonating just below the threshold of what the human ear can hear. Some research indicates that elephants can communicate with each other, even when separated by miles.

Spend a day among elephants and you will come away mystified. Sudden, silent, synchronous activities – a herd taking flight for no apparent or audible reason, a mass of scattered animals simultaneously raising their ears and freezing in their tracks – such events demand explanation, but none is forthcoming....

I stumbled on a possible clue to these mysteries during a visit to the Metro Washington Park Zoo in Portland, Oregon, in May 1984. While observing three Asian elephant mothers and their new calves, I repeatedly noticed a palpable throbbing in the air like distant thunder, yet all around me was silent.

Only later did a thought occur to me: As a young choir girl in Ithaca, New York, I used to stand next to the largest, deepest organ pipe in the church. When the organ blasted out the bass line in a Bach chorale, the whole chapel would throb, just as the elephant room did at the zoo. Suppose the elephants, like the organ pipe, were the source of the throbbing? Suppose elephants communicate with one another by means of calls too low-pitched for human beings to hear?

'The rumbles are the key to our story'

Half a year later the World Wildlife Fund, the Cornell Laboratory of Ornithology, and friends in the Cornell biology department helped me, Bill Langbauer, and Liz Thomas return to the zoo to test this idea. We recorded near the elephants for a month. Then we made electronic printouts and saw that we had recorded four hundred calls – three times as many as we'd heard.

Elephant sounds include barks, snorts, trumpets, roars, growls, and rumbles. The rumbles are the key to our story, for although elephants can hear them well, human beings cannot. Many are below our range of hearing, in what is known as infrasound.

The universe is full of infrasound: It is generated by earthquakes, wind, thunder, volcanoes, and ocean storms – massive movements of earth, air, fire, and water. But very low frequency sound has not been thought to play much of a role in animals' lives. Intense infrasonic calls have been recorded from finback whales, but whether the calls are used in communication is not known.

Why would elephants use infrasound?

It turns out that sound at the lowest frequencies of elephant rumbles (14 to 35 hertz, or cycles per second) has remarkable properties – it is little affected by passage through forests and grasslands. Does infrasound, then, let elephants communicate over long distances?

Suddenly we realized that if wild elephants use infrasound, this could explain some extraordinary observations on record about the social lives of these much loved, much studied animals. Iain and Oria Douglas-Hamilton, Cynthia Moss, and Joyce Poole, in their long-term studies of elephants in Tanzania and Kenya, had reported many examples of behavior coordinated by some unknown means over distances of three kilometers or more.

For instance, how do the male and female elephants find one another for reproduction? This was a question raised by Joyce's doctoral research on the lives of males. Adult males and females live independently from one another, moving unpredictably over a great territory, with no fixed breeding season. A male elephant spends part of each year in a condition called musth, when he crisscrosses large areas in an endless, irritable search for females in breeding condition. Well may he feel irritable, for receptive females are a truly scarce resource. With two years of gestation followed by two more of nursing, a female is receptive only a few days every four or five years.

But they do find one another. In fact, as Joyce observed, the amazing thing is that the female is no sooner in estrus than she is surrounded by males that gather from all directions….

How has the estrous female informed males from far and wide of her condition? The answer may lie in a unique sequence of intense, low-frequency calls that a receptive female makes during her estrus. This sequence always has the same form and thus technically may be called a song.

Slow, deep rumbles, rising gently, become stronger and higher in pitch, then sink down again to silence at the end. The performance may continue for half an hour, and before the day is out the singing elephant will be surrounded by male elephants.

Katharine Payne
'Elephant Talk'
National Geographic
August 1989

Friends to humans

Elephants, captured alive, allowed people better to understand and appreciate their qualities of sweetness, intelligence and anthropophilia. The affectionate beasts that Plutarch and Aelian described are similar to our present-day circus animals or those in Rudyard Kipling's fables.

Intimate elephant

Many anecdotes of antiquity have been preserved in the writings of Plutarch. That of the young flower seller has often been retold.

The loves of some animals are wild and furious, while others have a refinement which is not far from human and an intercourse conducted with much grace. Such was the elephant which at Alexandria played the rival to Aristophanes the grammarian. They were, in fact, in love with the same flower-girl; nor was the elephant's love the less manifest: as he passed by the market, he always brought her fruit and stood beside her for a long time, and would insert his trunk, like a hand, within her garments and gently caress her fair breasts.

Plutarch
Moralia, early 2nd century

Talented elephants in Rome

Aelian, one of the last authors of classical antiquity, born at the end of the 2nd century, borrowed essential details from his predecessors – from Aristotle to Plutarch. To these, he added personal observations or contemporary facts, many of them taken up again by writers of the 19th and 20th centuries.

Touching the sagacity of Elephants, I have spoken elsewhere; and further, I have spoken too of the manner of hunting them, mentioning but a few of the numerous facts recorded by others. For the present I intend to speak of their sense for music and their readiness to obey, and their aptitude for learning things which are difficult even for mankind, to say nothing of so huge an animal and one hitherto so fierce to encounter. The movements of a chorus, the steps of a dance, how to march in time, how to enjoy the sound of flutes, how to distinguish different notes, when to slacken pace as permitted or when to quicken at command – all these things the Elephant has learnt and knows how to do and does accurately without making mistakes. Thus, while nature has created him to be the largest of animals, learning has rendered him the most gentle and docile.

Now had I set out to write about the readiness to obey and to learn among elephants in India or in Ethiopia or in Libya, anyone might suppose that I was concocting some pretentious tale, that in fact I was on the strength of hearsay about the beast giving a completely false account of its nature. That is the last thing that a man in pursuit of knowledge and an ardent lover of the truth has any right to do. Instead I have preferred to state what I have myself seen and what others have recorded as having formerly occurred in Rome, treating summarily a few facts out of many, which nevertheless sufficiently demonstrate the peculiar nature of the beast.

The Elephant when once tamed is the gentlest of creatures and is easily induced to do whatever one wants. Now keeping due eye on the time, I shall state the most important events first. Germanicus Caesar was about to give some shows for the Romans. (He would be the nephew of Tiberius.) There were in Rome several full-grown male and female elephants and there were calves born of them in the country; and when their limbs began to grow firm, a man who was clever at dealing with such beasts trained them and instructed them with uncanny and astounding dexterity. To begin with he introduced them in a quiet, gentle fashion to his instructions ... [they] wheeled into a circle when he so ordered them, and if they had to deploy, that also they did. And then they sprinkled flowers to deck the floor, but with moderation and economy, and now and again they stamped, keeping time in a rhythmical dance.

Aelian
On the Characteristics of Animals, early 3rd century

Mister Elephant

The happy medium for stump-clearing is the lord of all beasts, who is the elephant. He will either push the stump out of the ground with his tusks, if he has any, or drag it out with ropes. The planter, therefore, hired elephants by ones and twos and threes, and fell to work. The very best of all the elephants belonged to the very worst of all the drivers or mahouts; and this superior beast's name was Moti Guj. He was the absolute property of his mahout, which would never have been the case under native rule: for Moti Guj was a creature to be desired by kings, and his name, being translated, meant the Pearl Elephant. Because the British government was in the land, Deesa, the mahout, enjoyed his property undisturbed. He was dissipated. When he had made much money through the strength of his elephant, he would get extremely drunk and give Moti Guj a beating with a tent-peg over the tender nails of the forefeet. Moti Guj never trampled the life out of Deesa on these occasions, for he knew that after the beating was over, Deesa would embrace his trunk and weep and call him his love and his life and the liver of his soul, and give him some liquor. Moti Guj was very fond of liquor – arrack for choice, though he would drink palm-tree toddy if nothing better offered. Then Deesa would go to sleep between Moti Guj's forefeet, and as Deesa generally chose the middle of the public road, and as Moti Guj mounted guard over him and would not permit horse, foot or cart to pass by, traffic was congested till Deesa saw fit to wake up.

There was no sleeping in the daytime on the planter's clearing: the wages were too high to risk. Deesa sat on Moti Guj's neck and gave him orders, while Moti Guj rooted up the stumps – for he owned a magnificent pair of tusks: or pulled at the end of a rope – for he had a magnificent pair of shoulders – while Deesa kicked him behind the ears and said he was the king of elephants. At evening time Moti Guj would wash down his three hundred pounds' weight of green food with a quart of arrack, and Deesa would take a share, and sing songs between Moti Guj's legs till it was time to go to bed.

Once a week Deesa led Moti Guj down to the river, and Moti Guj lay on his side luxuriously in the shallows, while Deesa went over him with a coir swab and a brick. Moti Guj never mistook the pounding blow of the latter for the smack of the former that warned him to get up and turn over on the other side. Then Deesa would look at his feet and examine his eyes, and turn up the fringes of his mighty ears in case of sores or budding ophthalmia. After inspection the two would 'come up with a song from the sea', Moti Guj, all black and shining, waving a torn tree branch twelve feet long in his trunk, and Deesa knotting up his own long wet hair.

Rudyard Kipling
Moti Guj – Mutineer

A Just-So story

'Seed the battery this mornin'?' said Ortheris. He meant the newly arrived elephant-battery; otherwise he would have said simply 'guns'. Three elephants harnessed in tandem go to each gun, and those who have not seen the big forty-pounders of position trundling along in the wake of their gigantic team have yet something to behold. The lead-elephant had behaved very badly on parade; and had been cut loose, sent back to the lines in disgrace, and was at that hour squealing and lashing out with his trunk at the end of the line; a picture of blind, bound, bad temper. His *mahout,* standing clear of the flail-like blows, was trying to soothe him.

'That's the beggar that cut up on p'rade. 'E's *must*', said Ortheris pointing. 'There'll be murder in the lines soon, and then, per'aps, 'e'll get loose an' we'll 'ave to be turned out to shoot 'im, same as when one o' they native king's elephants *musted* last June. 'Ope 'e will.'

'*Must* be sugared!' said Mulvaney contemptuously from his resting-place on a pile of dried bedding. 'He's no more than in a powerful bad timper wid bein' put upon. I'd lay my kit he's new to the gun-team, an' by natur' he hates haulin'. Ask the *mahout,* sorr.'

I hailed the old white-bearded *mahout* who was lavishing pet words on his sulky red-eyed charge.

'He is not *musth*', the man replied indignantly; 'Only his honour has been touched. Is an elephant an ox or a mule that he should tug at a trace? His strength is in his head – Peace, peace, my Lord! It was not *my* fault that they yoked thee this morning! – Only a low-caste elephant will pull a gun, and *he* is a Kumeria of the Doon. It cost a year and the life of a man to break him to burden. They of the Artillery put him in the gun-team because one of their base-born brutes had gone lame. No wonder that he was and is wrath.'

'Rummy! Most unusual rum', said Ortheris. 'Gawd, 'e is in a temper, though! S'pose 'e got loose!'

Mulvaney began to speak but checked himself, and I asked the *mahout* what would happen if the heel-chains broke.

'God knows, who made elephants', he said simply. 'In his now state peradventure he might kill you three, or run at large till his rage abated. He would not kill me, except he were *musth. Then* would he kill me before any one in the world, because he loves me. Such is the custom of the elephant-folk; and the custom of us *mahout*-people matches it for foolishness. We trust each our own elephant, till our own elephant kills us. Other castes trust women, but we the elephant-folk. I have seen men deal with enraged elephants and live; but never was man yet born of woman that met my lord the elephant in his *musth* and lived to tell of the taming. They are enough bold who meet him angry.'

Rudyard Kipling
My Lord the Elephant, 1902

A ride on the back of an elephant, as depicted in an early 19th-century Indian miniature.

An elephant with a mind of its own

From South India comes this tale of a very independent elephant named Kandakoran.

The forests of Kerala abound in herds of wild elephants. From time to time, an elephant may fall into a trap and be captured. Then begins the long, arduous and unrelenting work of training it. Once tamed, it is usually sold to a temple or a king.

Kandakoran, the hero of our story, was sold to the temple of Subramania in the city of Travancore.

He was an enormous, magnificent beast, one of the most beautiful

elephants that had ever been seen in Kerala.

His height harmonized marvellously with his massive bulk and made him a well-proportioned animal. His long, curved tusks thrust straight forward, leaning neither too much to the left or right. Even the way he held his head was majestic, and his ears, which were abnormally large, hung from either side of his jutting brow. In short, he possessed all the qualities that are the mark of an exceptional elephant.

Despite his size, he was sweet-tempered and never, it was said, in the course of his long life did he harm the smallest of creatures, even when he was rutting, and crazy juices swam through his temples. As everyone knows, each elephant has his own personality, and Kandakoran was no exception. He loved to do things his own way, and it was impossible to make him change his mind as he had a natural aversion for orders, no matter what they were.

The handlers who cared for him were aware early on of this character trait and became used to letting him act in his own manner, and as it seemed best to him. Unlike other elephants, Kandakoran was never tied up as he refused to submit to such an indignity. When night fell, he would choose a comfortable spot and stretch out.

Kandakoran loved to bathe in the river that ran nearby, north of the temple. He stayed out of the heat as much as possible, and when he was not working would pass the warm hours of the day in the water, at the spot where it was deepest. He became the faithful friend of the water buffalos, who would pass along the banks or splash in the pools not far from him. Sometimes,

during the dry season, the buffalos would no longer be able to find pastures to graze. Kandakoran could not bear to see his friends starve, above all when fields of sugarcane grew along the riverbanks, under their very nose. These fields were fenced in, and the buffalos could only look at them. But this was not an obstacle for Kandakoran.

One day, followed by the herd of buffalos, he left the river and, having soon made an opening in the fence, waited for his companions to eat their fill. The owners of the field arrived quickly, brandishing sticks to frighten away the buffalos, but as soon as Kandakoran saw them he charged upon them.

He was careful not to hurt anyone, but the peasants fled, frightened by his surges forward, seized with panic. When the buffalos had eaten to their hearts' content, Kandakoran escorted them back to the river and recommenced his interrupted swim. It was said that he never took a single stick of sugarcane for himself. And it is a fact that he was never seen to take any food not expressly intended for him.

Another time, Kandakoran was lazing in the river. A boat laden with ginger, coconuts and bananas was making its way downstream. Its cargo was so heavy that the rim of the boat was barely above water level. Kandakoran saw the boat but the bargemen did not see him, and their skiff landed on his back. As soon as this happened, he lifted his trunk and grabbed hold of

Preceding page and right: elephants at work in Siam in the early 19th century.

the boat. While its occupants, terrified, threw themselves into the current to swim to shore, Kandakoran tore the boat to pieces....

From that time on, the river folk bore some ill-will towards Kandakoran. And, as the feeling was mutual, never for the rest of his life did Kandakoran permit a boat to pass him whenever he was in the river.

If perchance a boat appeared, the elephant would move either upstream or downstream, depending, and smash it to pieces. Soon, it was necessary to re-route river traffic by several kilometres to avoid Kandakoran. The bargemen would even come down by foot to determine his presence or absence before starting their long, arduous journey. If he was there, they had to wait until he left. Many of them would bring offerings to Subramania temple in the hope that Kandakoran would be gone by the time they had to pass that spot in the river. Even today, one can see in the temple a row of lamps offered by bargemen on such occasions.

Kandakoran was considered the first elephant of the temple, and thus it was he who was designated to carry the idol in the processions on festival days. But on these occasions, it was not necessary for the handlers to disturb him. Because Kandakoran, as soon as he was aware it was time, would leave the river of his own accord and head for the temple. There, he would station himself under the large steeple of the golden temple and patiently await the attendants to come to adorn him with the traditional coiffure.

He would lift one of his back legs to let an attendant climb up on his back. The attendant would affix the idol

firmly, then climb back down again in the same manner. Kandakoran would never have permitted anyone ever to climb on to him from the front. The man holding the silk umbrella, the one who plied the fan of peacock feathers, and the attendant who span the fly-swatter of yak-tails, all clambered up on to him from behind.

The procession would take place in the inner precinct of the temple according to a precise deambulatory order and for a period of time fixed in advance. There was never any need whatsoever to guide Kandakoran: he would stop at the appropriate times and would move with all desired slowness. There was only one problem. If for any reason the authorities decided to speed up the ceremony, Kandakoran would not prove to be very cooperative. No force in the world could make him change his routine.

In this regard, it has been said that when Kandakoran led the procession it was impossible to cheat on the amount of oil put in the lamps, as the festival would always last the exact amount of time it was supposed to.

The last day of the ceremony, during the performances that would run late into the night, never would one see Kandakoran misbehave and fight with the other elephants; never did one see him run like a beast or frighten the crowd, taking advantage of a commotion. He always sat calmly, tranquilly, swinging his immense ears, as if he too was enjoying the entertainment.

One evening, the festivities had just ended, and Kandakoran was walking alone, as was his habit, searching for a place to stretch out for the night. As he

The elephant working as a beast of burden in early 19th-century Siam.

was on a badly lit, out-of-the-way road, an old woman, half-blind, walked all the way up to him without noticing him. Perceiving the elephant at the last moment, she started with fear and fell senseless to the ground, in front of his powerful feet. The attendants who were following her began emitting cries of terror and fled.

The road being too narrow for Kandakoran to push the old woman to one side, he stayed there, without moving. The woman finally came to her senses and pulled herself up, crawling away to the side. Then Kandakoran, kicking free the umbrella she had dropped on the road, started off again on his way.

Who has ever heard of an elephant as intelligent as that? Was he not the most marvellous elephant that ever existed?

When Kandakoran would haul the fully grown trees that grew in such vast quantity in Kerala, there was never a treetrunk too heavy for him. Yet, without his consent, it would have been impossible to get him to lift a mere stick.

For him to accept a job, it was necessary first of all to agree on a price, one part set aside for the temple, the other for his own use, in the form of food. The handlers would inform him of the size of the tree he was to move; they would tell him where he was to leave it, and the salary fixed for the job. If the deal appealed to him, he would trumpet his agreement, going to fetch the treetrunk and carry it to the designated spot. If he was not immediately given his portion of bananas, coconuts or sweets, he would pick the treetrunk up again and immediately haul it back to its starting point.

One day, a man arrived at the temple requesting his services to move an enormous tree. A price was agreed upon. Then the handlers asked the man:

'What do you intend to give to Kandakoran?'

'Ten bunches of bananas, ten coconuts and twenty pounds of molasses', the man responded, without hesitation.

When this proposition was communicated to Kandakoran, he trumpeted loudly to express his satisfaction and accomplished his task with diligence. The man then said that Kandakoran would receive his food several days later. Kandakoran immediately returned to the spot where he had just deposited the tree and moved it back to the place from which he had taken it.

Not knowing what to do, the man approached several other elephants, but their combined efforts were in vain: the tree would not move even the distance of a mustard seed. In the end, the man, completely vexed, went back to Subramania temple. A new deal was struck, and Kandakoran, who was taking his usual bath in the river, was called in. But he refused to obey at any price whatsoever.

There are many tales about the elephants of Kerala. Each has its own characteristics and personality but none has the free will of Kandakoran!

Of the influence of music on Hans and Marguerite, the two elephants of the Museum

In 1803 the Dutch East India Company donated two elephants to Holland. The couple soon became famous and attracted observers – scientific and otherwise – from far and wide. They were even the subject of a well-known book, the lavishly illustrated 'Natural History of the Two Elephants of the Museum'.

You demand, citizens, details of the concert given, on the tenth day of the ninth revolutionary month, to the Elephants in the botanical gardens; you want to know what effect music has on animals whose social instincts and habits are most worthy of exciting our curiosity.

I give thanks to those artists who, armed not with scalpels and instruments of torture, but with oboes, flutes and violins, came to ply the charms of their art on two beings gifted with feeling, to delight their natural senses, which captivity has enchained, to excite them, calm them by degrees, awake in

PARIQUI LA FEMELLE

HANZ LE MÂLE

" Barely had the first chords been sounded when Hans and Marguerite (for thus they are named) pricked up their ears and ceased eating; soon they hastened to the spot from whence came the sounds. "

their forest-spirit the instincts of their homeland, and to lead them, finally, through accents of joy and tenderness, to the illusion of a love that, in order to be fully gratified, needs no witnesses.

The concert began with a trio of short, varied airs for two violins and bass, in B major, of a sober character. Barely had the first chords been sounded when Hans and Marguerite (for thus they are named) pricked up their ears and ceased eating; soon they hastened to the spot from whence came the sounds.... The first worried movements were appeased when they saw that all remained calm around them; then, giving themselves over with no fear at all to the sensations of the music, they no longer received any impulse other than what it gave them.

The change in mood was most noticeable at the end of the trio, which

the players concluded with a dance air, in B minor, from *Iphigenia in Tauris* by Gluck, music of an untamed, emphatic character, which communicated all its rhythmic agitation to them. In their gait, sometimes speeding up, sometimes slowing, their movements at times brusque, at times slow and smooth, one would have said that they were following the undulations of the song and measure. Often, they chewed upon the bars of their stalls, squeezed them with their trunks, pressed against them with the whole weight of their bodies, as if there was not enough space for their gambols, and they wished to roll back the boundaries. At intervals, they emitted piercing cries, whistling; was this happiness or anger, the handlers were asked.

'They are not angry', was the response. This passion calmed, or at least changed its object, with the next air: *Oh, My Tender Musette,* played in the key of C minor, on solo bassoon, without accompaniment. The simple and tender melancholy of this romance, made even more plaintive by the melancholic tones of the bassoon, attracted them through a kind of magic spell. They walked several steps, stopped to listen, came and sat down beneath the orchestra, moving their trunks softly and seeming to inhale its amorous emanations....

But the spell did not exert itself equally on both. While Hans withdrew into his circumspect and prudent nature, Marguerite, passionate, caressing, stroked him with her long and flexible member, which she drew up and down across his back and along his neck, before bringing it back upon herself, pressing her own breasts with its 'finger'; and, as if this 'finger' were imbued with a feeling more urgent and tender by the minute, she put it first into her mouth, then in Hans' ear – but he was not listening, or perhaps did not know its language.

This silent scene suddenly assumed a fiery and disorderly character with the gay and lively pulse of the tune *Ça Ira,* played in the key of D by the whole orchestra, its effect particularly enhanced by the piercing tones of the piccolo.

Of their transports, their cries of ecstasy, sometimes low, sometimes high, but always of varied intonation; of their whistling, their comings-and-goings, you would have said that

❝ I give thanks to those artists who, armed not with scalpels and instruments of torture, but with oboes, flutes and violins, came to ply the charms of their art on two beings gifted with feeling. **❞**

"But the spell did not exert itself equally on both. While Hans withdrew into his circumspect and prudent nature, Marguerite, passionate, caressing, stroked him with her long and flexible member, which she drew up and down across his back and along his neck...."

the rhythm of this melody marching at double-time pressed them forward, spurred them without interruption, and forced them to move as it did. Thus the female redoubled her solicitations. Her caresses became even more demonstrative. Her flirtations became more pointed; often she would rapidly pull away from the male, then reversetowards him, giving him quick kicks in the behind so that he would not forget that she was there; but poor Marguerite got nothing for her troubles. Happily for her, though, the invisible force troubling her senses also had the power to calm them.

The instruments played no more, and she followed their lead steadily when, like those refreshing rains that dampen the fires of summer, the sweet harmony of two human voices rose from the orchestra like a magus to quieten her delirium. In the middle of her most active raptures, she was seen suddenly to rein herself in, to still her urges by degrees, and finally to stop motionless and drop her trunk to the ground. The repose whose image she reflected was that of an adagio from an opera by Dardasues, plaintive shades, sung by two voices and accompanied throughout in B flat.

Letter from the Citizen Toscan
in J. B. Houel,
*Natural History of the Two
Elephants of the Museum*,
1803

Grooming an elephant.

Sacred elephants

When Siam became Thailand, it lost the white elephant at the centre of its flag, which recalled the royal cult devoted to this rare albino animal. Burma and Laos had similar customs. This narrative recalls many others from the 17th and 18th centuries.

For more than a year, the White Elephant had been a cause of gravest concern to the emperor of Burma's inner circle.

Morose, unhappy, irritable, devoid of appetite, slowly and fatally wasting away, the thrice-sacred animal which for nearly eighty years had symbolized the supreme trinity – religious, military and civil – appeared to be gradually approaching his end.

In vain had all the allures capable of tearing His Lordship from his fatal torpor been heaped around him. To the fiefdom he already possessed as his own like a royal prince, and whose revenues were devoted to his upkeep, was added another fiefdom twice as large, whose riches were incalculable.

It was this act of largesse that made him the wealthiest lord of the empire. His *roon* (his minister, head of his household), convicted of some mildly shady goings-on – administrative and financial pecadillos – was delivered up to his lofty justice. The *S'hen-Mheng* (Lord Elephant), having sniffed disdainfully from the end of his trunk, was content to throw the minister on the ground, place his monstrous foot on his head, and crush it like an egg.

He did this with complete simplicity, with an air of brutal preoccupation, without even seeming to think about it, and without bothering the least with the niceties that usually accompany such 'replacements' of ministers.

Previously, he had possessed only a single driving-houk, in gold encrusted with gems, with a crystal handle encircled by rubies and sapphires: the emperor, forever generous, gave him a second one.

The cloth of his scarlet tiara, sparkling with huge rubies and marvellous diamonds, was replaced with a new one, and the emperor attached to it with his own august hand the famous spray of diamonds....

The 'circle of nine precious stones' meant to ward off evil spirits was never again absent from his forehead, and, for even greater safety, two new ones were added to each of his tusks. Each day he was clothed in full dress. On his head he wore, in the manner of Burma's high dignitaries and even the emperor himself, a golden plaque inscribed with all his titles; between his eyes glittered the famous cross in precious stones; on his ears hung enormous golden pendants; his magnificent caparison, made of scarlet bands of woven silk and gold, covered with pearls and gems, shone forth like the sun over his emaciated form; his favourite *mahouts* carried four golden umbrellas above him, and, so that he could admire his full splendour and savour the pleasures of his wealth, above his golden feeding trough was installed an immense mirror, sent expressly from a Saint-Gobain manufacturer, whose purchase and transport cost an exorbitant amount. Finally, this legendary golden trough was always full of tender grasses, exquisite shoots, delicious fruits, and over these the emperor, with the crazy prodigality of an oriental monarch, had had precious stones strewn.

All in vain! The lanky body of *S'hen-Mheng*, which was about 12 feet high, trembled on his fat, gnarled legs. His trunk hung sadly down between his enormous tusks; his shifty, disagreeable, and at times singularly cruel expression lived on frozen, as it were, in his eyes, which were red like an albino's. In short, he remained insensible to everything.

From time to time, and with difficulty, he chewed languidly on one of the thousand delicacies that his servants, his guardians, and his officers, all the way up to the emperor, offered him with superabundance.

All seemed to presage a catastrophe, and, even in the eyes of the least clairvoyant, it became obvious that His Highness *S'hen-Mheng* was going to die.

For those aware of the importance of this creature, the influence he had over all that was called Burma, people and things, it was clear that his death, which was approaching without his having been provided with a replacement, was the harbinger of the most horrifying catastrophes.

The emperor and his whole family would fall victim to the greatest misfortunes and most terrible calamities – plagues, earthquakes, flood, famine, would ravage the entire empire.

So, to ward off this formidable series of disasters, whose repercussions would be felt from the emperor all the way down to the lowliest of subjects, functionaries of every rank, grade and quality began to examine the smallest bits of evidence concerning the possible existence of a White Elephant that could be the heir to *S'hen-Mheng*.

They launched searches employing all means possible, sending at great cost expeditions to localities where there was even the barest hint of the presence of the sacred animal, as much to reassure the emperor and his dynasty as to earn the colossal fortune that would fall to the person lucky enough to find the White Elephant.

L. Boussenard
The Adventures of a Lad from Paris in the Land of the Tigers,
Travel journal, 1 November 1885

The pillars of the world

The 'Ramayana', sacred Hindu epic, exists in numerous versions from different eras and in various languages. The earliest, from the 5th century BC, is attributed to the poet Valmiki. It paints a general picture of the adventures of Rama, one of the incarnations of the god Vishnu. We hear about the city of Ayodya: 'Filled with violent elephants, elephants of colossal strength, large like mountains.'

In accord with the command of their royal Sire, the princes renewed their tunnelling and came upon the monstrous form of the elephant of the quarter, Virupaksha, who was supporting the earth with its mountains and forests on his head.

O Kakutstha, at a given moment, when that great elephant shakes his weary head, an earthquake results therefrom.

The sons of King Sagara, having circumambulated that immense elephant, protector of the quarter, by digging deeper came to Rasatala.

Having explored the eastern region, they went to the south, and in the southern quarter, they beheld another great elephant, the magnanimous Mahapadma, like unto a mountain, who held the earth on his head; and their astonishment was great.

Having circumambulated him, the sixty thousand sons of Sagara, of great soul, dug the western quarter; and in the region of the west, a great elephant, whose bulk exceeded the height of a mountain, named Saumanasa, appeared to them. Having paid homage to him and questioned him as to his welfare, they dug until they reached the region that contains the Soma.

In the north, O Illustrious Son of Raghu, they beheld Himpandura of noble stature, who supported that quarter, and, having circumambulated him, the sixty thousand princes hollowed out the earth with fury.

The Ramayana of Valmiki

Ganesh (opposite) and scenes of elephants in Indian miniatures (below).

African legends

Numerous African stories depict animals from an anthropocentric point of view: the panther is seen as crafty and cruel, the hippopotamus as thick-headed and restless. The elephant, generally portrayed as a wise and powerful king, is often the victim of crafty animals who take advantage of his pleasant nature, benevolence, lack of aggression and sense of fair play.

Song of the elephant

The images one finds here are those that often make up the subject matter of traditional African songs.

In the forest that weeps, in the wind of
  evening,
The night, all black, has gone to sleep,
  happy:
In the sky, the stars have fled,
  trembling,
Dim fireflies that shine on and off.
Above, the moon is dark, its white light
  extinguished.
Spirits wander.
Hunter of elephants, take your bow!

[Choir:]
Hunter of elephants, take your bow!
In the fearful forest, the tree sleeps, the
  leaves are dead,
The apes close their eyes, hanging from
  branches on high,
The antelopes glide with silent tread,
Eating fresh grass, pricking their ears,
  attentive,
Raising their head and listening,
  frightened.
The cicada goes still, silencing his crisp
  song.
Hunter of elephants, take your bow!

[Choir:]
Hunter of elephants, take your bow!
In the forest that the great rain lashes
Father elephant walks, heavy, baow!
  baow!
Heedless and fearless, sure of his power,
Father elephant, whom nothing can
  vanquish.
Among the trees that he breaks, he
  stops and goes again.
He eats, trumpets, overturns trees, seeks
  his female.

Young elephant shielded by its mother. Opposite: Another type of elephant-hunting weapon.

Father elephant, you're heard from afar.
Hunter of elephants, take your bow!

[Choir:]
Hunter of elephants, take your bow!
In the forest where nothing passes by but you,
Hunter! lift your head, glide, run, leap and walk.
Your meat lies before you, an immense slab of meat,
Meat that walks like a mountain,
Meat that makes the heart rejoice,
Meat you'll roast in your hearth,
Meat in which you'll sink your teeth,
Beautiful, red meat whose blood is drunk steaming.
Hunter of elephants, take your bow!

[Choir:]
Yoyo! hunter of elephants, take your bow!

Yoyo! hunter of elephants, take your bow!

Song recorded by R. P. Trilles
on the banks of the Abanga,
tributary of the Ogowe

A. Jeannin
Africa's Elephants, 1947

The battle between cunning and force

'Why do you always remind me that I'm small? On the other hand, I'm strong, more so than you think, and I'll prove it to you any time you want. Just know that I'm capable of crushing you, if I wish!'

'What's that?' exclaimed the Wise One of the bush, highly amused. 'Please repeat what you just said, because I didn't quite hear it.'

'You heard very well what I said! I

said I can crush you in front of everyone, any time you'd like!'

'Crush me? Me? When with the sole of my foot I can turn you into pulp like a tomato or throw you with my trunk above the woods as one would throw a pebble with a sling?'

'Very well,' said Tüb-Rawa the hare, 'I'll meet you on Sunday, in the middle of the clearing nearby. You will hear me shout from the kapok-tree, and there, in the presence of the entire village, I will challenge you.'

The day of the contest, all the village hurried to view the battle between cunning and force. Hare placed himself so that M'Ba Wogbo the elephant would approach through the cleft in the enormous kapok-tree, knowing full well what would happen. The monster of the kapok-tree seized the trunk of M'Ba Wogbo and twisted it. The elephant collapsed on the ground.

M. Colardelle-Diarassouba
*The Hare and the Spider
in African Tales*
1975

This legend tells how people learned that the river M'Gboti shelters a demon

Is it not God, the great Sky, who gave to M'Gboti, in creating it, the power to receive sacrifices? The Agni killed an elephant in Diamlabo, then they set off into the brush. The man went to kill the elephant, but the elephant fell into the M'Gboti water.

They shot at him from above with a rifle, then decided to go and cut him into pieces. There were a hundred of them; the first one that went was thrown back and fainted into the wake of his own red blood, you follow me? (repeat) And in this way ninety-nine

disappeared; one more and it would be a hundred. The last one sat down and said to himself: 'Ah, the group has been gone a long time, and I can't see them returning at the moment. I'm going back to the village.' And he went back to the village.

Nobody ever saw the ninety-nine men who had gone into the water return. 'If he goes, I go too', each one had said. And now, only one intelligent man was left. Sunset came, and he thought, 'Because of that, I'm not going into the water, I'll go to tell the village.' The villagers decided to consult the soothsayer. The latter said: 'That elephant was a *musu*. But the men killed it, and it went to seek refuge near the water.' It was because of the death of these men that the soothsayer was consulted, and it was because of his words that ever since, sacrifices are made to M'Gboti. That is the origin of the custom, in the early days, before the arrival of white men. Sunday, Monday and Friday, you can hear the 'drum-playing' down there, you can hear the trumpet, as if there were people.

Théophile Obenga
Mbochi Traditional Literature
1984

How the hare was made *mwene*, king of the animals

The animals were without a royal leader. They decided to find themselves one. To this end, they held a great meeting in the court of the Lion.

Some voted for the Leopard, but he was not selected because he feeds on the flesh of other animals. Others preferred the Lion because of the fearful respect he inspires. But the final choice was none other than the Elephant, the unanimous vote of all the animals. It was good that the entire country should have a single leader. Thus, a great Council of notables was called on *odua*, the day of rest, in the village of the Lion, to crown the elected chief, the elephant, in the presence of all the animals – those of the forest as well as of the savannas and marshes.

The Hare began thinking seriously about this matter.

The village of the Hare was situated on a plain close to that of the Lion. Thus it was that many animals passed through the Hare's village while travelling to the Lion's, and on the way they asked the Hare: 'Friend, why are you not ready yet?' The Hare's reply was, invariably: 'My wife is still cooking manioc and sorrel for me, because we are spending several days where we are going. In the meantime, not all our friends have yet passed through!' And the Hare's response satisfied them.

But then the Hare placed himself on the Elephant's path, sick to the point of dying, with a huge, churning stomach, eyes sunk into their cavities, tongue hanging out. Nonetheless, he found enough voice to say to the Elephant: 'You see my condition, and there is nobody to carry me. So, I am forced to stay at home.' To which the Elephant, with a compassionate gaze, replied, 'Friend Hare, my very dear friend, you know that I have always depended on you. It would be unthinkable that you should stay here while I was being crowned king of all the animals. Come, I'll carry you on my back.'

So the Hare climbed on the back of the Elephant, and, across mountains and valleys, the Lion's village was soon in view. At this moment the Hare, the suffering invalid, said to his bearer:

'Now walk serenely!' All the animals greeted the entry of the Elephant, hailed him with veneration, the Hare still on his back. The illness of the Hare magically disappeared as he acknowledged the cheers of the animals, smiling away on the back of the Elephant.

When the moment of the official investiture arrived, the Hare said to the Elephant: 'It's I who should be crowned, since you carried me on your back. And while I was there, I waved to all the other animals. Do you doubt my word? Ask them!' All the animals agreed that it was true. The Elephant was crestfallen.

Thus it was that the Elephant was not made king in front of the Council of notables in the presence of all the other animals, due to the intelligence of the Hare. Having tricked the Elephant, the Hare was made *mwene*.

Théophile Obenga
Mbochi Traditional Literature
1984

The theme of the elephant as victim of the hare is repeated in many Indian fables.

On the battlefield

The image of elephants that has most captivated the imagination of the 19th and 20th centuries is that immortalized by Hannibal: the elephant as beast of war, as assault vehicle.

In 242 Carthage fell victim to the famous Mercenary revolt immortalized by Gustave Flaubert in his novel 'Salammbô'. Hamilcar 'Barca', a Carthaginian general and Hannibal's father, observes the horrible losses experienced by his stable of elephants.

These animals were the pride of the great Punic houses. They had carried the elders, triumphant in war, and they were worshipped as the favourites of the sun.

Those of Megara were the strongest of Carthage. Hamilcar, before leaving, had made Abdalonim vow that he would look after them. But they had died from their mutilations; and only three remained, lying in the middle of the court, in the dust, in front of the debris of their feeding-trough.

They recognized him and came to him.

One had ears horribly split, the other, a large wound in his knee, and the trunk of the third was cut off.

However, they looked on him with an air of sadness, like reasonable people; the one who no longer had a trunk, lowering his enormous head and bending his hocks, tried to stroke him gently with the hideous end of his stump. As the animal caressed him, two tears came to his eyes.

A part of the Barbarian army, able to escape from one of Hamilcar's traps, falls upon the Numidian elephants of his ally, Narr' Havas.

Among the undulations of these hillocks, sheaves the colour of silver shone, separated one from another; the Barbarians, dazzled by the sun, perceived, with some confusion, the great black masses below supporting them. These rose, as if they were blooming. They were lances in towers on the elephants, which were terrifyingly armed.

Besides the pikes on their chests, the bodkin tusks, the bronze plaques that covered their flanks and the daggers attached to their kneecaps, they had at the end of their trunks a leather bracelet through which the handle of a large cutlass had been inserted; having departed at the same time from

the back of the plain, they advanced on both sides, in parallel.

A nameless terror froze the Barbarians. They did not even try to flee. Already they found themselves enveloped.

The elephants entered into this mass of men; the spurs on their chests divided it, the lances on their tusks overturned them like ploughshares; they cut, hewed, hacked with the scythe of their trunks; the towers, full of phalarae, seemed like volcanoes on the march; all that could be seen was a large mass in which human flesh made white spots; pieces of brass, grey sheets; and blood, red rockets; the horrible animals dug black furrows as they passed through the middle of all this. The fiercest was driven by a Numidian crowned with a diadem of feathers. He hurled javelins with frightening speed, all the while emitting a long, high-pitched whistle at intervals; the huge beasts, docile like dogs, kept an eye on him throughout the carnage.

Their circle narrowed little by little; the Barbarians, weakened, did not resist; soon the elephants were at the centre of the plain. There was not enough space; they thronged, half-rearing, together; they locked tusks. Suddenly, Narr' Havas quieted them, and wheeling around they returned to the hills at a trot.

Two groups, however, hidden at the right in a fold of the earth, had thrown away their weapons and, on their knees facing the Punic tents, they lifted their arms to ask for mercy. Their legs and hands were tied; when they were stretched out on the earth next to one another, the elephants were led back.

Chests cracked like boxes being broken; each of the elephants' steps crushed two; their great feet sinking into the bodies with a movement of their haunches made them seem to limp. They continued and went on until the end.

Gustave Flaubert
Salammbô
1862

The Shah-nameh

Here is a message from King Saweh of Turkey to Bahram, the Persian ruler, as the two are about to join battle.

'If I cause my army to advance, they will hinder ants and flies from passing: then, I have a thousand elephants covered with armour, before whose smell knights' horses take flight. Who, in Turan or in Iran would dare present themselves before me, hoping to give me trouble with their arrival?…

Renounce this battle and come to me, I will not make you stand long before me, I will give you power and my daughter; I will give you honours and a diadem.'

After the refusal of Bahram, the battle takes place, at first to the Persians' disadvantage.

King Saweh said to his nobles: 'Lead the elephants to the front of the army, have the troops advance en masse to combat.'

When Bahram spied the elephants from afar, he became worried, drew his sword and said to his nobles: 'Oh illustrious and valiant men! Prepare your bows, place your helmets on your heads. I implore, by the life and head of the king of the world who is elected by the nobles and the crown of men of good, all those who have a bow and arrows to draw their bows now, to hit the trunks of the elephant with an arrow of poplarwood thirsty for blood and with triple wood, and to seize your clubs, to go into combat and to exterminate the enemy.…'

The stars were obscured by the feathers and points of the arrows. They pierced the elephants' trunks with their darts, and the valleys and the plains became like a sea of blood.

When the elephants felt themselves wounded by the points of the arrows, they trampled their own army underfoot, they turned their backs to escape the wounds and crossed the whole stretch of the battlefield: the army followed them.

Many men died in this procession, many others were trampled to death by the elephants, and not one in ten returned home.

Firdawsi
The Book of Kings
11th century

Previous page and right: elephants at war, from engravings of 1715.

African journey

François Levaillant, who travelled across Africa from 1781 to 1794, is best known for having brought the first giraffe back to the French king. Occasionally during his travels he took part in elephant hunts.

We didn't lose sight of our animals' tracks for a single moment

After several hours of fatigue and arduous hiking through brambles, we arrived at an open, wooded spot. For a large area there was nothing but bushes and a few copses of trees. We stopped. One of my Hottentots, who had climbed a tree to observe, after having cast an eye in all directions, signalled to us, placing a finger to his lips, to keep quiet; he indicated, by opening and closing his hand several times, the number of elephants he saw. He climbed down; we deliberated, and we took the leeward direction in order to approach undetected. He led me so close, through the undergrowth, that he brought me face to face with one of these enormous animals. We were, you might say, touching each other; yet I did not see it! not because fear had transfixed my eyes; it was necessary to give one's full attention and to prepare for danger; I was on a little hillock below the elephant itself. My brave Hottentot tried as best he could to point at it, and repeated twenty times with an impatient, hurried tone…. THERE IT IS! LOOK, THERE IT IS!… I could not see it at all; my gaze fell a little farther on, as I was unable to imagine that what lay twenty paces below me was anything other than a lump of rock, because the mass was entirely immobile. Finally, however, a slight movement caught my attention. The head and tusks of the animal, which blotted out his enormous body, turned anxiously towards me. Without losing any more time or my advantage in lofty contemplations, I placed my large gun on its swivel and let fly a shot which landed in the middle of his forehead.

He fell dead. The noise immediately caused about thirty others to scatter, fleeing as fast as their legs could carry them. Nothing could be more amusing than to see the movement of their great ears thrashing the air in time to the speed of their running: this was naught but a prelude to an even more animated scene.

I was watching them with pleasure when one passed alongside us who had received a gunshot wound from one of my people. From the excrement tinted with blood that was pouring from him, I surmised he had been seriously wounded; we started to follow him. He would lie down, get up again, fall back down; but still on his heels, we brought him up again with our gunshots. The animal led us through the high undergrowth that was strewn here and there with the trunks of overturned dead trees. On the fourteenth gunshot, he turned, furious, on the Hottentot who had fired on him; another aimed a fifteenth shot, which only increased the elephant's rage; and coming up beside us, he shouted at us to watch out. I was but twenty-five paces away; I was carrying my gun, which weighed thirty pounds, not including my ammunition. I was not in as good a position as my people who, not having let themselves stray as far, had that much of a lead on me to escape the vengeful proboscis and get out of harm's way. I fled; but by the instant the elephant gained on me. More dead than alive, abandoned by my own (only one man was running over at that moment to defend me), I felt the only course left was to lie down and huddle against the thick trunk of an overturned tree; I had barely done so when the animal arrived, leaping over the hurdle; and, himself quite afraid of

the noise of my people he heard in front of him, he stopped to listen. From my hiding place, I could easily have shot him; luckily my gun was loaded; but the beast had already received so many blows in vain, and he was in such an awkward angle from where I was that, despairing of being able to bring him down with one shot, I remained motionless, awaiting my fate. I observed him, however, resolving to fight for my life if I saw him come towards me. My people, worried about their master, called from all sides. I refrained from responding. The terrified elephant retraced his steps forthwith and jumped a second time over the treetrunk, six paces below me, without having noticed me; at that moment, I stood up again, in my turn hot with impatience, and wanting to signal to my Hottentots that I was alive, sent a bullet into his rump. He disappeared entirely from view, leaving everywhere, on his path, clear traces of the cruel state in which we had put him....

However, night approached; we hastened to find the elephant I had had the good fortune to kill with a single shot

There was nothing more for us to do in the matter; our presence scared away some vultures and several small carnivores who had lost no time and had already started to take the first bites. We built several fires; supplies were lacking. My people grilled some meat for themselves from the elephant; they prepared for me some portions of the trunk. I ate it for the first time, but I swear it will not be the last, because I have never found anything so exquisite. Klaas assured me that once I had tasted the feet I would soon forget the trunk;

to convince me, he promised to have a delicious breakfast prepared for me the next day.

So the elephant's four legs were cut off; a hole of around three or four square feet was made in the ground. This was filled with live coals; and, once everything had been covered with very dry wood, a large fire was kept burning part of the night; when it was judged to be hot enough, it was emptied out; Klaas then put in the animal's four feet and had them covered up again with hot cinders, then with coals and brushwood, and this fire burned until day.

All that night, I slept alone; my people kept guard; such was Klaas' order. I was told that they had heard many buffalos and elephants prowling around us. We were expecting that; the

"My people grilled some meat for themselves from the elephant; they prepared for me some portions it will not be the last, because I have never found anything so exquisite."

whole forest was full of them, but the multiplicity of our fires had prevented them from bothering us.

My crew presented me with an elephant's foot for breakfast

Cooking had made it swell up enormously; I could barely recognize the form; but it was so attractive, emitted such a pleasant aroma, that I

of the trunk. I ate it for the first time, but I swear

hurried to taste it; it was indeed a meal fit for a king; whatever praise I have heard about bears' feet, I could never imagine how an animal as heavy and fleshy as the elephant could produce so fine, so delicate a dish. 'Never,' I said to myself, 'no, never have our modern-day Luculluses been able to grace their tables with such a morsel as I have at hand at this moment. In vain does their gold convert and overturn the seasons; in vain they boast of being able to put all regions into service; their wealth does not compare to this; it is beyond the limits of their greedy sensuality'; and I devoured without bread the foot of my elephant; and my Hottentots, seated beside me, regaled themselves with other parts they found no less excellent.

These details may appear puerile, or completely without interest, to the majority of readers; it is necessary to tell everything, as until now people have had only bizarre notions or absurd fictions about the country I travelled through.

We used the rest of the morning to pull off the tusks; as it was a female, these barely weighed twenty pounds; the beast was eight feet three inches tall. My people weighed themselves down with all the meat they could carry, and we began the route back to camp. We had considered following the trail of the animal who had spared my life and whom we had so cruelly mistreated; but so many others had come during the night that the tracks were confused. Besides, we were so fatigued, and I feared so to overtax these poor people! I led them back as quickly as possible....

Journey by F. Levaillant through the African Interior via the Cape of Good Hope, vol. 1

The Bastille's elephant

*Where are you going now?',
Montparnasse resumed.*

*Gavroche pointed to his
two young charges and said:
'I'm going to put these two
children to bed.'*

'Where?'

'At my place.'

*'Your place? Where's
that?'...*

*'In the elephant', said
Gavroche.*

Montparnasse, despite his unflappable nature, could not refrain from exclaiming: 'The elephant!'

'Well, yes, in the elephant', Gavroche replied. 'Swhat?'

This is a word in a language nobody writes and everybody speaks. 'Swhat?' means: And what's the matter with that?

This profound observation on the boy's part restored Montparnasse to calm and good sense. His estimation of Gavroche's lodgings seemed markedly to improve.

'Well I never!' he said. 'Of course, the elephant. Is it comfortable?'

'Very', said Gavroche. 'There are no draughts like under the bridges.'

'How do you get in?'

'I just do.'

'So is there a hole?' Montparnasse asked.

'Of course! But don't tell anyone. It's between the front legs. The cops haven't seen it.'

'And you climb up? I understand.'

'In a jiffy, crick, crack, and it's done, not a soul to be seen.'

After a silence, Gavroche added: 'For these little ones I'll get a ladder.'

Montparnasse began to laugh.

'Where the devil did you get those brats?'

'A wigmaker made me a present of them.'

We call it a monument although it is nothing more than a maquette. But this maquette itself, a magical rough draft, a grandiose cadaver of an idea by Napoleon, which two or three successive gusts of wind had carried and tossed each time a little farther away from us, had become historic and had taken on something indefinably definitive that was in direct contrast to its provisional appearance. It was an elephant, forty feet high, made of a wooden frame covered with masonry, and carrying on its back a tower resembling a house; originally painted green by some housepainter, it was now painted black by the sky, rain and weather. In this deserted, open corner of the square, the broad forehead of the colossus, its trunk, its tusks, its tower, its enormous rump, its four legs like columns, created, at night, against a starry sky, a surprising and terrible silhouette. It was hard to know what it meant. It was some sort of symbol of popular strength. It was sombre, enigmatic and immense. It was one knew not what kind of powerful ghost, standing visible alongside the invisible spectre of the Bastille.

Few strangers visited this edifice; nobody passing it looked at it. It had fallen into ruin; with each season, the mortar, pulling away from its sides, created hideous wounds. The 'town fathers', as one might say in polite usage, had forgotten it since 1814. It was there in its corner, gloomy, ill, crumbling, surrounded by a rotting railing constantly soiled by drunken coachmen; a network of cracks fingered their way up its belly, a slat of wood jutted out from its tail, high grasses grew between its legs; and as the level of the square had risen around it over the past thirty years due to that slow, continuous movement that insensibly raises the soil of large cities, it stood in a hollow, and it seemed as if the earth had emptied itself out under it. It was huge, despised, repulsive and superb, ugly to the eyes of the bourgeois, melancholy to the eyes of the thinker. It had something about it resembling a piece of rubbish that one might sweep away,

and something of a king who was about to be beheaded.

As we said, at night its aspect changed. Night is the true milieu of all that is shadowy. As soon as twilight fell, the old elephant became transfigured; it took on a tranquil and terrible form in the formidable serenity of darkness. Being of the past, it was of the night; and obscurity went well with its grandeur.

This monument that was rude, squat, heavy, harsh, austere, almost deformed, but certainly majestic and imprinted with a sort of magnificent and savage gravity, has since disappeared. In its place peaceably reigns a sort of giant stove adorned with its stove pipe, replacing the sombre, nine-towered fortress almost as the bourgeoisie replaces feudalism....

Arriving close to the colossus, Gavroche understood what effect the infinitely large can produce on the infinitely small, and said: 'Kids! Don't be afraid.'

Inside the elephant

It was a lair open to those to whom all other doors were shut. It seemed that the old, miserable mastodon, invaded by vermin and neglect, covered by warts, mould and ulcers, rickety, worm-eaten, abandoned, condemned, a sort of colossal beggar asking in vain for the handout of a benevolent gaze in the middle of the square, had itself taken pity on another beggar, the poor pygmy who went about without shoes on his feet, a roof over his head, blowing on his fingers, dressed in rags, fed on scraps. Here was the purpose of the Bastille elephant. This idea of Napoleon's, disdained by the people, had been taken up by God. That which had only been illustrative had become august. For the Emperor to have realized what he imagined, it would have taken porphyry, brass, iron, gold, marble; for God, the old assemblage of planks, joists and plaster was enough. The Emperor had had an inspired dream; in this titanic elephant, armed, prodigious, holding his trunk erect, carrying his tower, making joyous and vivifying waters spout up all around him, he wanted to incarnate the people; God had made of it something even grander: he housed a child inside.

The hole through which Gavroche had entered was a crack barely visible from the outside, hidden, as we said, under the belly of the elephant, and so narrow that only cats and children could barely scrape through.

'Let's begin', said Gavroche, 'by telling the porter that we're not in.'

And plunging into the darkness with

Plan for the elephant fountain at the Place de la Bastille.

the certainty of one who knows his apartment well, he took a board and covered the hole.

Gavroche went back into the darkness. The children could hear the sputtering of the taper in the bottle of phosphorous. The chemical match did not yet exist; the Fumade tinder box at that time represented progress.

A sudden light made them blink; Gavroche had just lit one of the strings soaked in resin that are called cellar-rats. The cellar-rat, which smoked more than it illuminated, made the interior of the elephant dimly visible.

Gavroche's two guests looked around them and felt something similar to what someone shut up in the great barrel of Heidelberg might experience, or even better, what Jonah must have felt in the biblical belly of the whale.

Victor Hugo
Les Misérables, 1862

'The Roots of Heaven'

In 1980, shortly before his violent death, Romain Gary published the definitive edition of his book 'The Roots of Heaven'. Interpretation of the title depends on whether the author is speaking through Morel, defender of the elephants, or Waïtari, head of a nationalist group, who, to finance its struggle, ends by massacring the great ivory bearers.

From Chad to the Cape, the African's voracious appetite for meat, eternally preoccupied as he was by famine, was what the continent had most strongly and most fraternally in common. It was a dream, a hankering, an aspiration of every moment – a physiological cry more powerful than the sex instinct. Meat! It was the most ancient, most real, most universal aspiration of humanity. He thought of Morel and smiled bitterly. For the white man, the elephant had for a long time been uniquely for ivory, and for the black man, it was uniquely for meat, the most abundant quantity of meat that the lucky hit of a poisoned assegai could procure for him. The idea of the elephant's 'beauty', the elephant's 'nobility', was a notion of the satisfied man, the man of restaurants, two meals a day and museums of abstract art – a view of the elitist spirit that, faced with the hideous social realities it is incapable of confronting, takes refuge in the lofty clouds of aesthetics, intoxicating itself with vague and crepuscular notions of beauty, of the 'noble', of the 'fraternal', simply because the purely poetic attitude is the only one that history allows it to adopt. Bourgeois intellectuals demand that their decadent society encumber itself with elephants, for the sole reason that they hope thus themselves to escape destruction. They know they are as anachronistic and cumbersome as these prehistoric beasts: it is a simple way of crying for pity for oneself, in order to be spared. Such was the case with Morel – a typical case if ever there was one. It was much easier to make elephants a symbol of liberty and human dignity than to translate these ideas politically and give them real content. Yes, it was truly easy: in the name of progress, one demands a ban on hunting elephants and then admires them tenderly on the horizon, one's conscience tranquillized in having thus rendered to each man his dignity. One flees from the action but takes refuge in the gesture.

It was the classic attitude of the western idealist, and Morel was a perfect example of it. But for the African, the elephant had no other beauty besides the weight of its steaks and, as for human dignity, that is above all the matter of a full belly. Or at any rate, that is where it starts. When the African has a full belly, perhaps then he too will become interested in the aesthetic side of the elephant and give himself over to pleasant meditations on the beauties of nature in general. For the instant, nature advises him to open the belly of the elephant, to sink his teeth into it, to eat, eat himself into a stupour, because he never knows where the next morsel is coming from. But this is a matter that there was no question of discussing openly. For the moment, Marxism itself was a difficult luxury. The new nationalisms had everything to gain in the short term by locating themselves in the terrain of decadent bourgeois sentimentality, in which the 'beauty of ideas' was often a decisive argument, rather than of historical materialism, which aimed at the bourgeoisie in its guts. Thus he had done his best to annexe the protection, the 'respect' for elephants and all the actions of Morel. But the sentimentalism of the western crowds surpassed everything that he knew of it: it was necessary to stop the equivocation that hid from the eyes of the world its importance to him, Waïtari. And also to procure the funds indispensable to putting a serious organization on its feet. He had twenty men in three trucks, all armed and equipped; none of them had been paid.

Romain Gary
The Roots of Heaven
1980

Stills from the film version of *The Roots of Heaven*, directed by John Huston, 1958.

Elephant hunting in Africa, 1920.

Towards protection

On 6 December 1905 the Society of the Friends of the Elephant was founded in Paris. The director of the Natural History Museum brought together such celebrities as the composer Camille Saint-Saëns, then at the height of his fame.

This association has as its primary goals to stop the terrible annual slaughter of elephants, to regulate the traffic in ivory and, in our African territories, to spread the domesticization of these proboscidians which are ideally equipped to render immense services in colonization and transportation.... The fate of this animal threatens to be the same as that of the dronte and the oepyornis; it may soon be included on the list of extinct species.

Perrier
Director of the Museum
President of the Society of
the Friends of the Elephant

The dilemma of the African elephant, *c.* 1906

Although the question does not exactly lend itself to laughter, nonetheless we should not discourage good humour by taking an overly ponderous attitude. The little song 'Friends of the Elephant' with which Paul Hippeau enlivened the association's first banquet uses doggerel to do a pretty good job of summing up for us the group's aims, attitudes and ideas.... One must not forget that in the colonialist and capitalist ambience of the day, the essential argument made on behalf of the elephant concerned its utility and profitability; this was the

Ivory market.

sole means to interest the powers that be and politicos. The West today is more sensitive about these issues and has progressively moderated its opinion on the problem of ivory trafficking.

Friends of the Elephant

The elephant, it's a notorious fact,
In Africa is disappearing.
If we don't hasten to look at that,
How can we remedy it?
The elephant is a friend to man;
More than the dog, it's constant.
And now indeed our turn has come
To be the friend of the elephant.

In all the lands of Africa,
The elephant is everywhere hunted;
From Congo to Mozambique
Against him the Negro is allied;
To traffic in his tusks
He is wickedly put to death.
And now the time has come in France
To be the friend of the elephant.

While the Negro in full fury
Treats them with brutality,
In India they appreciate
Their strength and their docility.
In early days, Pyrrhus, king of Epirus,
At war was excellent.
The Romans had themselves slain
By this staunch friend of the elephant.

This intelligent pachyderm
Can be turned to good advantage
As much as a cow on a farm.
You can make good use of it.
It can carry fantastic loads
And make a child happy.
It takes the place of a servant.
Let's all be friends of the elephant.

Many enlightened souls
Have long pondered this question

And searched in what manner
One might find a good solution.
The moment seems favourable
Modestly to suggest
That you agree as you leave your table
To be a friend of the elephant.

Let's protect their future destiny
And stand up in their defence.
Otherwise, the two Guineas
Will have no more of them by
tomorrow.
It's one of the kings of nature,
This interesting beast,
So save the future breed,
You, the Friends of the Elephant.

Camille Saint-Saëns champions elephants' rights

To this panegyric, full of the naïve postulates of the period, one might add another by one of the most widely known figures among the non-specialists solicited, Camille Saint-Saëns (1909).

The matter of elephants is not my area of competence; nonetheless it has preoccupied me for a long time. What advantage there would be in possessing a beast of burden like this instead of being followed by an army of porters!

And how much better than to sacrifice these superb animals to turn their tusks into billiard balls....

It is true that a lot of money can be made for a time, and that it has made people act like those savages who slaughter a tree to have its fruits, without thinking of the future. The extermination of important species is a deplorable thing to which intelligent people should, in my humble opinion, oppose themselves with all their power.

The mammoth: back in service

Since the ban on the trade of African ivory, manufacturers have made plans to import mammoth tusks.

This was the decision taken by the majority of two-thirds of the representatives of the 103 countries who met in Lausanne [Switzerland] in October 1989. Their ruling would be put into effect at the end of three months. This historic decision, hammered out after years of delays, had immediate repercussions on world markets. In Paris, for example, those rare boutiques where ivory goods are still made and repaired saw a dramatic rise in their business.

'People suddenly became aware of the value of the ivories they possess', explains Pierre Heckmann, whose family has run a stall in the sixth arrondissement for three generations. 'They brought them to me to be repaired. Certain clients even asked me to sculpt busts of them in ivory. I'm working sixty hours a week.'

Prices in antique shops went wild. An antique chess set that a year before was

worth FF 40,000 [£4000] recently sold for FF 400,000 [£40,000] at Sotheby's in London.

On the other hand, the market in Africa for elephant tusks plummeted. It was announced that raw ivory, which not long ago was selling for FF 1,200 [£120] per kilo, now brings no more than FF 400 [£40] in Zaire. Merchants in Africa and Asia, especially Hong Kong, who built up dozens or even hundreds of metric tons of stock are wondering to whom they are going to sell from now on.

Those countries that, like Taiwan or the Ivory Coast, were not among Lausanne's '103 club' can be counted on one hand and will likely have their trade particularly carefully watched. The tens of thousands of artisans and merchants who, around the world, work and trade in ivory are questioning themselves about their future. They know the substitutes, many of which have been around for a long time: the Galalith and celluloids that were fashionable decades ago and the resins of today, as well as bone, Japanese deer antlers and even corozo, that 'vegetable ivory' produced by an Amazonian palm tree. But these ersatz materials can never replace the superb whitish substance of elephant tusks. So what is left are the tusks of mammoths....

Precious pachyderms

These early giants, hump-shouldered and covered with hair, grazed along the steppes of the Northern Hemisphere. They sported enormous, curved tusks, some of which weigh as much as 125 kilos each. The Neanderthal, and later Cro-Magnon tribes who hunted them for food tricked them into ditches, where they would perish. Even then,

their ivory served as a medium in which statuettes were sculpted, such as the Venus discovered in Lespugue [France] dating back some 25,000 years. But, for reasons still not fully understood, these precious pachyderms vanished off the face of the earth after less than fifteen centuries, around 10,000 BC.

All that remains of them are those engravings that, by the hundreds, decorate the walls of sacred caves, or their skins, buried in the soil. Several dozen specimens, more or less intact, have been recovered from the frozen mud of the Siberian permafrost. The most spectacular, seated upright on his enormous behind, is the pride of a' St Petersburg museum. The Muséum of Paris also has the good fortune to possess a shrivelled fragment of a mammoth head, which is always deeply impressive to visitors.

The graveyards of Siberian mammoths

The most common mammoth remains are bones, among which are included, naturally, tusks. Carried in bulk by gigantic Siberian rivers and deposited in the bends of rivers, this debris accumulated into veritable cemeteries. One of these has produced up to 8000 bones and dozens of tusks belonging to 120 individual animals.

These deposits have long been exploited. Prehistoric Ukrainians made use of these massive, indestructible relics to build their huts. Later, Alexander the Great was well aware of what was then known as 'ivory mined from the earth', to distinguish it from elephant tusks. The prospecting of, work and trade in this 'natural resource' has long been a factor in the economy of Siberian tribes. The throne of one of the Tartar emperors was entirely sculpted from the tusks of mammoths.

The conquest of Siberia by the Cossacks in the 17th century breathed new life into this ancient trade. French artisans remember their fathers working Russian ivory, which was regarded as a cheap substitute for African ivory at that time.

Indeed, the mammoth tusks preserved in the permafrost deepfreeze have survived through centuries with little damage. As long as they are in a humid location, they are not very different from present-day tusks, except for a thicker 'skin', a slightly coarser texture and their larger size. 'Even examining them under the micro-scope,' explains Heckmann, 'you really need to be an expert to tell them apart.'

It is unclear what the Soviet reserves of fossil ivory are today

They themselves admit that they are 'major', and that searches for new deposits continue. Already, wild rumours are circulating. In the United States and Canada, the price of mammoth tusks is said to have risen from $300 per kilogram to $800 in a few months. In this case, the Soviets possess a fabulous treasure that they must be even more tempted to cash in on, given their shaky economy. Their policy of non-exportation of raw ivory is on the brink of changing. Three years ago, through the discreet mediation of some Finns, they offered several tons of tusks to various French merchants. Several months ago, it was to the West German tablemakers of the Odenwald valley, threatened with closure, that they offered a market providing an annual supply of a ton of fossil ivory. The

Japanese immediately pricked up their ears.

In 1988 they had imported nearly 106 tons of African tusks for use in making piano keys, and above all those personal seals that are the rage over there. The latest thing is to have one's signature carved on a stick of ivory. Two million seals were produced last year.

After the ban

How is this industry to be supplied now that trade in ordinary ivory is finished? Why not buy Siberian mammoth ivory in bulk? In the face of a rise in the market and the rush towards their reserves, the Soviets seem to be reconsidering their position. What they plan to propose to a Japanese delegation preparing to leave Tokyo is the creation of a joint enterprise for the manufacture of ivory seals. It would be financed at least partially by Japanese capital but would remain in Yakut and employ local artisans.

Already the protectors of elephants are rising up in protest. Fossil ivory is not protected under any international law. Could such trade serve in fact to mask an illicit market for African ivory? Will this pillage of an irreplaceable palaeontological legacy also prolong that of a living and renewable resource? That would be absurd. In France, a forgotten decree from the Ministry of Agriculture, dated 12 March 1950, has been exhumed. It says that only elephant tusks can be sold as 'ivory'. That of the mammoth must do without this prestigious label.

Marc Ambroise-Rendu
Le Monde, 10 January 1990

Mammoth remains from Alaska.

Out of Africa

In ten years, the continent has lost at least half its elephants. How can the massacre be stopped? By banning trade, says a majority of countries. By organizing it, says Zimbabwe.

J uly 1989: The president of Kenya burns 12 metric tons of ivory.

Silently, slowly, with its curiously elastic walk, the elephant heads towards the locust tree. Virile and solitary, fanning itself with its large ears, its belly still wet from the nearby river, it harvests some of its favourite fruit using its expert trunk. A vision of Africa, wild and free. However, several kilometres to the south, large farms are producing tons of grain which they stockpile in ultramodern silos. And immense herds of cattle recall that Zimbabwe furnishes the European community with excellent meat. Another image of Africa. The country would like to preserve both.

The entire world mobilizes. Africa mourns its elephants. They disappear inexorably, massacred by poachers hungry for ivory. Zimbabwe is the exception: there are 52,000 animals today, compared to 30,000 ten years ago.

Guth, 35, a consultant for safari organizers, spends his life in the bush. Seated on a bank of the Zambezi, natural border with Zambia, in the Mana Pools National Park, he says 'The growth in population and the new

farmers' need for land relegate animals to restricted areas. These ought to be managed like model farms.' He explains the necessity for 'culling', in which professionals slaughter surplus animals – including elephants – en masse and as quickly as possible, in order to reestablish the equilibrium of an artificial ecosystem: a practice that is regularly labelled barbarous by animal lovers in the West. Tirelessly, Guth repeats the importance to his country of the foreign currency brought by tourism and hunting – if they are carefully regulated. 'A time will come', he says, 'when ecology is no longer confused with sentimentalism.'

A legacy of Anglo-Saxon colonialism, the national parks cover a tenth of Zimbabwe's area. Since independence in 1980, the new government has maintained, as well as it can, a conservation policy. The country is happy about these nature preserves in which animal-kings, protected from humans by laws and weapons, live in artificial paradises delimited by paper borders. As with many white Zimbabweans, safari organizers, hunters, or former hunters, Guth is proud of these parks that zigzag through his country, of the large safari districts... and of the elephants. And he firmly believes that if ivory loses its value, the elephant will not survive in Africa. Zimbabwe sees its herds growing regularly. Elsewhere, however, except in South Africa and Botswana, the elephant is threatened by obliteration. Between 1979 and 1989 its population fell from 1.34 million to 625,000. East Africa lost 52 per cent of its elephants in ten years. Kenya, which in 1973 possessed over 130,000, today harbours no more than 16,000. The

number of mature males able to reproduce – the special targets of poachers due to the length of their tusks – has shrunk, putting the survival of the species in peril. And for each female killed, a calf of less than two years will die as well, incapable of surviving alone.

The cause of carnage: ivory

A material that is mythical, immortal, that people have sculpted for millennia. The appetite of Asians, Americans and Europeans for this semi-precious substance is responsible for the death of thousands of elephants each year. In 1976 the animal was placed on the endangered species list by the countries who are signatories to the Washington convention. But the Convention on International Trade in Endangered Species (CITES), entrusted since 1986 with enforcing the quotas assigned to each country according to the size of their herd, proved itself impotent against poachers. International networks of traffickers were able to evade surveillance. The channels for ivory were re-routed. After Taiwan, Singapore and Macao, it was Dubai that served as the nexus of activity. In Africa, the corruption of government officials, the military and the police has enabled the export of ivory by means of false documents, sometimes via complicit countries such as the Republic of South Africa, which thereby inflated its exports. In other countries, the elephant trade has underwritten the costs of political conflicts. Tusks served as items of exchange for weapons. Today, Angola has no more than a skeletal herd of 1600 head.

The price of ivory continues to climb

In 1979 a kilogram was worth $63. In 1986, $260. A recent report by the International Union for Conservation of Nature and Natural Resources (IUCN) estimated this fruitful commerce over the last ten years at $50 million per year. Ironically, Africa profits from only a fraction of this manna from heaven – between $10 and 20 million. The rest lines the pockets of a handful of exporters, businessmen from Hong Kong or Tokyo.

Horrified by the slaughter seen last spring, Western countries decided to ban the import of ivory, whether raw or processed, into their borders. A brilliant move supported by a good number of non-governmental ecological organizations, such as the powerful World Wildlife Fund. And by certain African countries, alarmed at having to stand by and watch impotently the obliteration of their elephant population. In June 1989 seven countries – among them, Kenya, Tanzania and Somalia – also demanded a ban on ivory trade.

But the controversy divides the continent. On one side, East Africa – led by Kenya and Tanzania – supported by the European Economic Community, the United States and the majority of ecological organizations, militates for a total protection of elephants. On the other, southern Africa, suspected of cooking its figures, embarrassed by the involvement of South Africa, requests an exception to the rule.

Zimbabwe, spearheading the efforts of southern Africa, refutes the arguments of Western ecologists. 'Just because Kenya or Tanzania can't manage their wildlife, we shouldn't be made to suffer', says the minister of tourism and wildlife, in the mauve shadow of the flowering jacarandas bordering the long avenues of Harare. But he has just lost the battle. In Lausanne the 103 countries adhering to the convention decided, on the 17 October, to suspend all ivory trade. His last hope: that experts will review southern Africa's situation. Will this measure suffice to save the elephants? No, the IUCN agrees, if African countries cannot provide the means to fight corruption and poaching.

But in Zimbabwe clearly nothing can be done without the support of the residents of the countryside. For villagers, this animal is often nothing more than a pest, capable of ravaging a field of sorghum in a night. Bob Monroe, of the Zimbabwe Trust, an association that tries to involve villagers in wildlife conservation, smiles bitterly: 'Did you "protect" your bears or your wolves, you [Westerners], when you were developing your agriculture?'

'To assure its place, the elephant must pay its way', asserts Ephraim

Chafesuka, president of the Guruve district, in the Zambezi valley. Zimbabwe decided to entrust to the villages near the national parks the management of, and hence the revenues from, their wildlife. It was their fields that the free-ranging animals were ravaging. Each year, an estimate of the surplus of animals is made with the aid of experts. Then, the district pays professional hunters, and the meat goes to villagers. A simple idea dating back to the sixties: wildlife is a renewable resource which, well managed, can bring more revenue than cows. An idea difficult to communicate in a land where cattle are still items for barter and symbols of affluence.

'Poaching becomes impossible'

With the ivory auctions at Harare, the distribution of meat to inhabitants, the revenue from tanning of the hides and above all the organization of safaris for foreign hunters – a tourist has to spend at least FF 150,000 [£15,000] to kill an elephant already condemned by the quota policy – the district earned

FF 750,000 [£75,000] in 1988 – an unheard-of figure in a region of chronic malnutrition. 'Before,' states Chafuseka, 'my village poached and risked prison to bring a wild animal into captivity. The animals were the property of the state. Today, they are our heritage. When an elephant is killed in the district, everybody knows. Poaching has become impossible.' So will Zimbabwe, ahead of its neighbours, be penalized? Or will it continue, as it threatens, to sell its ivory with the complicity of several Asian countries? That would be a catastrophe, ecologists protest, equivalent to 'providing an opening through which the rest of Africa can pour its contraband ivory'.

What is the solution? On the road from Makuti to Kariba, far from the preserves, in the Zambezi valley, vast stretches of savanna bear the scars left by giants. Will they be left to proliferate, even if ivory loses its value?

Corinne Denis
L'Express
27 October 1989

A 'hygienic' killing in Zimbabwe.

FURTHER READING

Adams, Jack. *Wild Elephants in Captivity.* 1981

Aelian. *On the Characteristics of Animals.* Trans. A.F. Scholfield. 1958

Bahadur, K. P. *A History of Indian Civilization.* 1983

Barrett, Norman. *Elephants.* 1988

Basham, A. L. (ed.). *A Cultural History of India.* 1984

Bazé, William. *Just Eephants.* Trans. H.M. Burton. 1955

Bell, Walter D. *Wanderings of an Elephant Hunter: African Collection.* 1989

Bere, Rennie. *The African Elephant.* 1966

Bertrand, Gabrielle. *A la recherche des éléphants sauvages.* 1960

Blond, Georges. *The Elephants.* Trans. Frances Frenaye. 1959

Bosman, Paul, and Anthony Hall-Martin. *Elephants of Africa.* 1988

Bright, Michael. *Elephants.* 1989

Buss, Irven O. *Elephant Life: Fifteen Years of High Population Density.* 1990

Carrington, Richard. *Elephants.* 1958

Cork, Barabara. *Elephants.* 1989

Delort, Robert. *Les Animaux ont une histoire.* 1984

Deraniyagala, Paul E. P. *Elephas Maximus: The Elephant of Ceylon.* 1951

Douglas-Hamilton, Iain and Oria. *Among the Elephants.* 1975

Douglas-Hamilton, Oria. *The Elephant Family Book.* 1990

Eltringham, S. K. *Elephants.* 1982

Fiasson, J. *Au Laos avec mes hommes et mes éléphants.* 1961

Fish, Byron, and George W. Lewis. *Elephant Tramp.* 1955

Gucwa, David, and James Ehmann. *To Whom It May Concern: An Inquiry into the Art of Elephants.* 1985

Hill, William C. O. *The Elephant in East Central Africa.* 1953

Hogan, Paula Z.. *The Elephant.* 1972

Holder, Charles F. *The Ivory King: A Popular History of the Elephant and Its Allies.* 1972

Jeannin, Albert. *L'Eléphant d'Afrique.* 1947

— *Les Bêtes sauvages et leur histoire: l'éléphant.* 1968

Keller, O. *Die antike Tierwelt.* 1913

Kipling, Rudyard. *Kipling's Kingdom.* Ed. Charles Allen. 1987

Selected Prose and Poetry of Rudyard Kipling. 1937

Künkel, Reinhard. *Elephants.* 1982

Lane, Margaret. *The Elephant.* 1985

Marshall, Sir John H. *Mohenjo-Daro and the Indus Civilization.* 1931

Moss, Cynthia. *Elephant Memories: Thirteen Years in the Life of an Elephant Family.* 1988

Osborn, Henry F. *Proboscidea.* 2 vols. 1936 and 1942

Penny, Malcolm. *The Elephant.* 1990

Petty, Kate. *Elephants.* 1989

Pfeffer, Pierre. *The Long Life and Gentle Ways of the Elephant.* 1987

Plutarch. *Moralia.* Trans. W.C. Helmbold. 1957

Pratapaditya, Pal. *Elephants and Ivories in South Asia.* 1981

Redmond, Ian. *The Elephant in the Bush.* 1990

Renou, L. *La Civilisation de l'Inde ancienne.* 1981

Rosny, J. H. *Quest for Fire.* 1982

Royston, Angela. *The Elephant.* 1989

Scullard, H. H. *The Elephant in the Greek and Roman World.* 1974

Sikes, S. K. *The Natural History of the African Elephant.* 1971

Smith, Sir Gratton Elliot. *Elephants and Ethnologists.* 1924

Stigand, Chauncey H. *Hunting the Elephant in Africa.* 1985

Stridworthy, John. *Elephant.* 1986

Sukamar, R. *The Asian Elephant: Ecology and Management.* 1990

Tournier, G. *Les Eléphants.* 1909

Toynbee, Jocelyn M. *Animals in Roman Life and Art.* 1973

Valmiki, Shri. *The Ramayana of Valmiki.* Trans. Hari Prasad Shastri. 1962

Williams, Heathcote. *Elephants.* 1986

— *Sacred Elephant.* 1989

Williams, J. H. *Elephant Bill.* 1950

Zeuner, Frederic. *History of the Domesticated Animal.* 1963

LIST OF ILLUSTRATIONS

INDEX

Figures in italics refer to pages on which captions appear.

PHOTO CREDITS

Archiv für Kunst, Munich 49, 50–1, 53*b*, 56–7, 81*a*, 82–3, 84–5, 92, 104*b*, 121*a*, 172–3. Gallimard Archives 19, 29*a*, 38, 47*b*, 70, 108–13. Artothek, Munich 22. Bibliothèque Nationale, Paris 26–7, 30–1, 33*b*, 39, 40, 45*b*, 46, 60–5, 74, 128, 147, 148, 150, 152, 155, 159, 161, 164–5, 176. Bios/Seitre, Paris 24*a*. B.P.K., Berlin 15*a*, 18–19, 122*a*, 123, 134. Bridgeman Art Library, London 28–9, 59, spine. British Library, London 11, 72, 89*a*, 89*c*, 89*b*, 100. Charmet, Paris 12, 16–17, 35, 45*a*, 53*a*, 57*a*, 97, 137, 145. L. Christophe, Paris 170, 171. Dagli Orti, Paris 78*b*, 80*b*, 88, 104–5. De Hugo, Paris 14–15. Edimédia, Paris 42, 73, 102–3, 169. Gamma, Paris 124–5. Giraudon, Paris 41, 52–3*b*, 75, 78*a*, 90–1. Jacana, Paris 132. Künkel, Munich 13, 23*a*. Magnum/Lessing, Paris 86–7. Michaud, Paris 2–9, 25*b*, 47*a*, 157, back cover. Musée de l'Homme (Photo Collection)/Lemzaouda, Paris 69*b*. Musée de l'Homme (Photo Collection)/Oster, Paris 116. Musée des Beaux-Arts, Lille 78–9. Muséum National d'Histoire Naturelle (Library), Paris 23*b*, *32*–3, 33*a*, 48, 53*a*, 66*a*, 67*a*, 68–9, 71, 74, 115*a*, 116–17, 118–19, 129, 146, 154. Muséum National d'Histoire Naturelle (Palaeontology Laboratory Photo Collection)/Serette, Paris 24*b*, 25*a*, 117, 131. Photothèque Albert Kahn, Boulogne 42–3, 43*b*. Rapho, Paris 66–7, 138–9, 141, 143, 149. Royal Geographical Society, London 94–5. Réunion des Musées Nationaux, Paris 76–7, 80*a*, 81*b*. Scala, Florence 20–1, 37, 44, 93, 107, 117, 120, 121*b*. Ronald Sheridan, Paris 77. Sipa, Paris 126–7, 182, 185. Tapabor, Paris 21*a*, 96*a*, 96*b*, 98. Today, Paris 183. Viollet, Paris 99, 101, 114, 123*a*, 130, 158, 162, 166, 178, 181.

ACKNOWLEDGMENTS

Grateful acknowledgment is made for use of material from the following works: Aelian, *Aelian*, vols. 1–3, trans. A. F. Scholfield, Harvard University Press, Cambridge, Mass., 1958. Reprinted by permission of the publishers and The Loeb Classical Library ('Talented Elephants in Rome'). Kipling, Rudyard, *Selected Prose and Poetry of Rudyard Kipling*, Garden City Publishing Co., Garden City, New York, 1937 ('Moti Guj'). Payne, Katharine, 'Elephant Talk', *National Geographic*, August 1989 ('The Language of Elephants'). Plutarch, *Moralia*, vol. 12, trans. W. C. Helmbold, Harvard University Press, Cambridge, Mass., 1957. Reprinted by permission of the publishers and The Loeb Classical Library ('Intimate Elephant'). *The Ramayana of Valmiki*, trans. Hari Prasad Shastri, Shanti Sadan, London, 1962 ('The Pillars of the World').

Robert Delort, M.Sc., Ph.D.,
has taught mediaeval history at the
Sorbonne, Paris, and the University of Geneva.
He has published many works on the Middle Ages.
His book *Les Animaux ont une histoire* (1984),
which deals with the subject of zoo history,
has been translated into several languages,
including Romanian and Japanese.
His current research topic is ecohistory,
or the history of the environment.

© Gallimard 1990

English translation © Thames and Hudson Ltd,
London, and Harry N. Abrams, Inc., New York,
1992

Translated by I. Mark Paris
Documents translated by Carey Lovelace

Printed and bound in Italy by
Editoriale Libraria, Trieste